BRUCE LEE:

THE INCOMPARABLE FIGHTER

Editor: Jack Vaughn
Art Director: Sergio Onaga
Cover Design: Michael Hitchcock and Sergio Onaga
Photos courtesy of Linda Lee
and Rainbow Publications, Inc.

Seventh printing 2003

OHARA 🔲 PUBLICATIONS, INCORPORATED
Santa Clarita, California.

by M. Uyehara

**To my wife, Chris
and
To my mother, Toki**

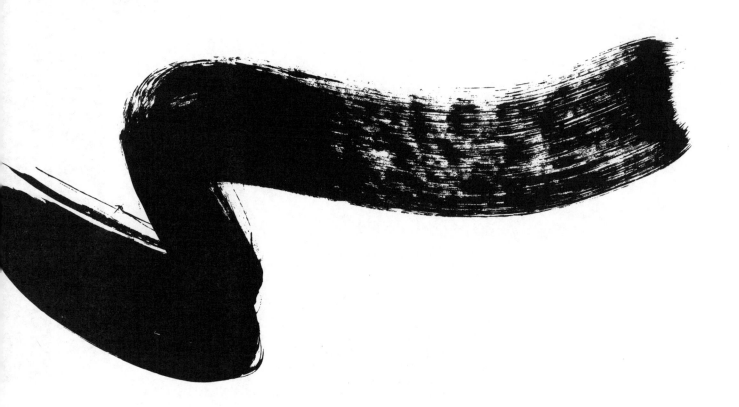

ABOUT THE AUTHOR
M. Uyehara was a personal friend and student of Bruce Lee.
These are his memoirs of the Bruce Lee he knew.

ACKNOWLEDGEMENTS

A book like this is not a creation of one person's judgment but of a number of opinions. I would like to thank all those who directly or indirectly contributed toward the making of this book.

My special thanks to Jhoon Rhee for briefing me about Bruce Lee during his stay with the superstar in Hong Kong. To Hayward Nishioka, the former National AAU Judo Champion and a karateka, for contributing his insight of Bruce Lee's prowess in the martial arts.

I would also like to thank Grace Lee, the actor's mother, who provided me with her son's background during his early years in Hong Kong. To Ted Wong and Herbert Jackson for sharing with me the many hours of studying jeet kune do at Bruce's home.

My sincere thanks to Linda Lee and Adrian Marshall for letting me use photos of the late actor, some of which have never been published before.

I'd also like to thank the staff at Rainbow and Ohara Publications who worked so hard in putting this book together.   *M.U.*

INTRODUCTION

When people see me, they always ask how good was Bruce Lee in the martial arts? "Was he as good as he was in his films?" or "Did he use a stand-in?" They always want to know what kind of person he was.

Those who didn't know the actor personally would sometimes comment stupidly, "I heard that he was only good in movies—actually even a brown belt could beat him."

Many top martial artists who knew him personally would not give him any credit for his prowess because by doing that, they'd think they were demeaning themselves. Others didn't like him because he was not the most tactful person. Bruce liked to prove his skill in many confrontations and he would not hesitate to embarrass others.

Bruce was good and he knew it, too. He became good because he put his heart and soul into the martial arts. He was not an ordinary fighter, he always felt that there was a way to develop more power and more speed in his punching and kicking.

He felt that Caucasians had an advantage over the Orientals because they were normally bigger. But he believed that this could be overcome by more training and better techniques. He saw the shortcomings of kung fu so he developed his own jeet kune do. He began to use techniques from boxing, foil-fencing and other fighting forms.

Wherever feasible, he adopted these techniques but he also improvised on his own. He was very creative and smart; he was able to combine all these different techniques so they blended completely into an art without any flaws.

He believed that all workouts must be done with intense physical and mental energy. "Hit the bag as hard as you can!" he used to say. "Just don't hit the surface, concentrate as hard as you can and imagine your fist going through the bag. At the same time rotate your hips, that's where your power is."

He used to emphasize that anyone who keeps hitting the bag a million times without mental intensity is just wasting his time. "Punching the bag without any feeling is just a waste. You have to hit from within your guts, otherwise your blow will never have power."

I am asked if another Bruce Lee will come along someday. Probably, but that person would have to think and focus all his attention on fighting. He would have to be a fanatic about fighting like Bruce was.

Since meeting Bruce in 1966 and being in touch with him until his death, I must admit that there aren't many who are like him. He was so creative and so obsessed with the martial arts that if he saw any flaw in his fighting method, he would spend hours trying to correct it.

What confounds me most was that he could do a technique or a movement like "broken rhythm" so smoothly. But when my friends or I tried to do it, we'd look completely awkward. He sure had a knack of making a difficult technique become simple.

M.U.

TABLE OF CONTENTS

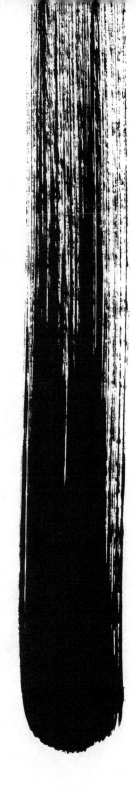

Bruce Lee in a familiar stance.

Why He Studied Kung Fu

1

On the cold, blustering day of November 27, 1940, Mrs. Grace Lee gave birth to her fourth child in San Francisco. Her husband, Hoi Chuen Lee, a Chinese opera singer, was not present as he was touring on the East Coast with his troupe from Hong Kong.

The parents named their son "Jun Fan" which meant "ever or always San Francisco," but his anglicized name, "Bruce," was given to him by the doctor who delivered him. Years later, the name "Bruce Lee" became a household word throughout the world. Ironically, it never dawned on anyone, especially the parents, that their son would someday become a legend, worshiped by millions.

When Bruce was about five months old, he and his parents returned to Hong Kong. There the hot and humid weather affected Bruce and he became very sick and weak. His mother had to constantly look after him, "I think I spoiled him because he was so sick," said his mother, Grace. "As he grew older, he got better . . . he was sometimes too active for me."

In his early years, Bruce was transferred from one parochial school to another because of his constant fighting, even though his teachers, according to Grace Lee, seemed to like him. Long after Bruce had left school for the U.S. he was still remembered as "Bruce, the bully and troublemaker."

Being a skinny kid, Bruce reminisced, "I always fought with my gang behind me. In school, our favorite weapon was the chains we'd find in the cans (toilets). Those days, kids improvised all kinds of weapons—even shoes with razors attached."

To Bruce, Hong Kong seemed to be a city of ghettos, everyone trying to make a living and no one getting anywhere. To belong to a gang was a natural tendency among the youngsters. "I only took up kung fu," Bruce confided, "when I began to feel insecure. I kept wondering what would happen to me if my gang was not around when I met a rival gang."

Bruce explained that many juvenile hoodlums and punks took up kung fu but didn't remain with it long. "They didn't take up the art for health or for disciplinary reasons—many of the students and even the instructors were on opium. My group stuck with kung fu just to learn to fight them."

Bruce as a child in Hong Kong.

According to Bruce, the martial arts clubs of that era were small and did not have united organizations like in Japan or the U.S. Each school was autonomous. The only contact with another club was when there was a challenge. The contest was usually held on a roof of a tall building to discourage any spectator or police interference. Normally, the contest was between students from two different styles.

"Like the old tradition, one school would challenge another," Bruce recalled, "and a designated time and place would be set. On the day of reckoning, each school would have its instructor and students to cheer the fighter on. Impromptu rules would be established, but those rules would be so minimal that the fight would be just about all out. Nobody really got hurt because the techniques weren't that effective. Guys would have torn shirts and bloody noses, but I never saw anybody really get hurt badly enough to have to go to the hospital."

Bruce with his mother, Grace, and his father, Hoi Chuen.

These contests were not really grudge fights, Bruce explained, but contests to find out which was the more superior among the styles of kung fu. After the battle, the fighters would shake hands and all parties would go to a restaurant for some tea.

Bruce never mentioned entering any of these contests but, according to his brother Robert, he got into a fight once when he was about 17 years old and got a black eye.

Robert also revealed that Bruce had studied several styles of kung fu but selected wing chun. "Bruce felt it was the most effective style then."

Bruce also told me that he had practiced tai chi chuan a few times when he was younger. His father used to get up early in the morning for the ritual and Bruce accompanied him. "I got tired of it quickly. It was no fun for a kid. Just a bunch of old men," he chided.

Bruce related that once he hurt a tai chi instructor on purpose. "I was about 15 and was getting disgusted seeing old tai chi men putting on demonstrations—having guys come up from the audience to punch their stomachs. One day while I was watching this demonstration, I didn't like the way this old man smiled when the young volunteer couldn't hurt him. When the old man asked for another volunteer, I went up. The old man, smiling, exposed his stomach as the target. But instead, I deliberately let go my right as hard as I could toward his ribs. I heard a crack as the old man crumbled to the floor moaning. You know I was such a smart-assed punk, I just looked down at the old man and laughed, "Sorry, I missed. Next time don't show off."

With a few years of wing chun behind him, Bruce became so confident of his skill that he entered an amateur boxing contest. "I hadn't had any training in boxing," he admitted, "but decided to enter because I thought I was pretty good in wing chun and that there wouldn't be much difference between my art and boxing. I never put on the gloves before, and it sure felt funny when I got into the ring. I learned to hit straightforward in wing chun, and that's what I did, knocking down my opponent," Bruce was declared the Hong Kong high school champion.

Bruce never mentioned it to me, but I later learned that he also captured the high school cha cha championship that year. Unless he thought it was important or if he still participated in that sport or activity, Bruce would not discuss it.

Bruce liked to wear fancy clothes while growing up in Hong Kong. "My parents were not real rich but we never had to worry about food or clothing," Bruce recalled. "We owned several apartments, and the rental income plus my dad's earnings from the opera brought in enough money to support our family of five children and two servants."

Bruce's slick dressing indirectly got him into a fight one night. He told me, "I was riding on this ferry late one night, and these two punks began to tease me. 'Are you a boy or a girl? You sure dress like a girl.' They kept teasing me, but I kept my cool and didn't say a word. But as soon as the ferry docked, I followed them ashore and started to swear at them. The bigger guy came after me, but I kicked him in the shin before he could do

Bruce hams it up on the dance floor.

8

anything. While he was jumping up and down hollering in pain, I went for the other guy, but he took off like a scared rabbit."

Although Bruce attended Catholic schools during his childhood, he wasn't religious at all. He could recite the Bible by heart but never discussed religion with anyone. It's possible that he received so much religion as a youngster, he shut himself completely off from it. Instead, Bruce turned to Chinese *Taoism* and other Oriental philosophies as well as to his jeet kune do and to his acting. Come to think of it, he just applied his whole life around the philosophies.

According to Bruce, most kids in Hong Kong hated cops. They were constantly harassing the kids. Bruce related, "Yeah, I didn't like the cops and the British. Damn cops! They thought that wearing those uniforms made them gods. The Chinese (cops) were even worse. They're the ones that patrolled the streets. We didn't see too many bobbies (British cops), they were usually the high-ranking officers.

"The cops in Hong Kong never talk to you politely. They treated the kids, and even the Chinese people, like dirt. Every time a cop opened his mouth, he'd swear at you. But if you were a white person, then he'd treat you completely opposite—he'd be polite, bowing and smiling."

Bruce said the people who were brought up in Hong Kong didn't like the British. "They were the ruling class. They were the minority but they ran the city. They lived up on the hills with big cars and beautiful homes, while the rest of the population, who lived below, struggled and sweat their asses to make a living. You saw so much proverty among the Chinese people that eventually it was natural to hate the filthy-rich British. They made the most money and had the best jobs just because the color of their skin was white."

Bruce with small friends

Bruce always had great rapport with youngsters. During his co-starring role in the *Green Hornet*, he was bombarded with invitations to attend parades or other events where children usually congregate. He loved to kid around with them and sign autographs. One of his favorite tricks was to place a dime in the hand of an unsuspecting boy or girl. "You can keep the dime if you are faster than me," he would encourage the youngster. "But before I take it away from you, I want you to have some practice." He would place the dime in the child's outstretched hand and then tell him to close his hand before he could take it. The first couple times, he would take the dime and say, "You're too slow. Let's try it one more time." On the next attempt, the child would gleefully exclaim, "I've got it! I've got it!" only to find, upon opening his fist, that the dime had been replaced with a penny. Bruce's movements had been so swift that the youngster hadn't even noticed the switch.

Early days training.

Early Years in the U.S.

2

To Bruce Lee, fighting was an important part of his life. Since he was a kid, learning kung fu was part of his culture, not unlike the American youngsters who learn to play baseball, football or basketball. Even today, kids still practice kung fu because fighting and violence are common in heavily populated Hong Kong.

Consequently, growing up in such an environment had a big influence on Bruce. He became an advocate of the concept that man should learn to defend himself. Whenever someone questioned Bruce's time spent in practicing the martial arts, he would counter with a few questions himself: "Are you a good driver?"

If the answer was affirmative, he'd ask the next question: "Do you carry insurance on your car?"

If the answer was again affirmative, he'd then reply, "Why do you need it, if you're a good driver?"

Generally, the response would be, "Because I don't know who's going to hit me."

"Ah ha!" Bruce would quickly point out. "You don't know who's gonna hit you, huh? Well, isn't this true in life? You never know who's gonna pick on you. You don't know when you'll get mugged. If it makes sense for you to carry insurance on your car, why not on your life? After all, you can always replace a car but not your life."

That was Bruce's way of avoiding an argument. He would have been a good salesman because of his sharp wit.

Like many Chinese immigrants, Bruce's first destination was San Francisco because of its large Chinese population. It seemed almost natural, somehow, that all Chinese should stop at 'Frisco first. But unlike most of them, he continued on to Seattle, Washington, a highly unlikely place to settle for an Oriental kid who could hardly speak English. Besides, its Chinatown was too small.

A city with just over half-a-million population with temperatures that average from 33 degrees Fahrenheit in the winter to 75 degrees in the summer, Seattle was quite different from his home. Named after an Indian chief, Seattle was icy and wet during most of the winter and comfortable throughout the rest of the year.

Hong Kong was extremely hot during the summer months and cool during the winter, although the average low temperature was only 61 degrees. Hong Kong's high humidity of 90 percent can cause extreme discomfort on a hot day. And its winter winds can send shivers to your body as they pierce through your heavy clothing. Then, there are the typhoons that sweep through the islands during the fall and winter months.

Hong Kong has a dense population of four million with 98 percent Chinese, even though the colony has been under British rule since the mid-1800s. Even today, the spoken language is still a Cantonese dialect.

With over 400,000 squatters still living in deteriorated huts or on fishing junks, the city is portrayed as dingy, disorderly and awfully over-crowded, compared to Seattle with its neat streets, well-kept buildings

Bruce teaching class at the Seattle kwoon.

and well-dressed citizens.

Seattle seemed to die at dusk in those days. Even before the sun sets, the shops and buildings begin to close their doors. Before midnight the streets are empty as the city has gone to sleep. In Hong Kong, however, the city stirs and becomes alive as soon as the sun is swallowed by the horizon. As darkness clothes the unsightly huts and dilapidated buildings, a metamorphosis takes place. Gaudy neon lights garnish the city. The reflections of the lights upon the calm sea color the whole scene—like an exotic city found only in travel books. Women of the night gradually emerge into the open, each one seeking a mate for the evening. All night long brazen music from clubs blasts through the city as if to compete against the cacophony coming from the horns of taxicabs which keep zipping through the streets.

It must have been a frightening experience for a young boy like Bruce to be placed in a strange city filled with people who were bigger and different. For the first time he was now a minority. But he also experienced good times, too: he enjoyed seeing snow fall for the first time, he liked being written-up in a newspaper after he had returned a lost wallet to its rightful owner, and he met Linda Emery, who later became his wife.

The only reason Bruce came to live in Seattle was because of Ruby Chow, a prosperous restauranteur who was a family friend. She offered him room and board in exchange for Bruce's labor as a waiter and dishwasher. But after a few months, self-reliant Bruce became disenchanted as he still had to rely on his parents for his miscellaneous expenses. He wanted to be self-sufficient because all his life he was considered the black sheep of the family.

"When I left Hong Kong, I promised myself that I'd not depend on my parents for any kind of help, and here I was getting money from them," he told me.

Soon Bruce started to teach his style of kung fu, called *wing chun*. During the day he attended Edison Technical High School, at night he worked at the restaurant and in between—including weekends—he taught a small enthusiastic group the art of kung fu. The training area was anywhere he could find privacy. Sometimes it was in a student's backyard. Other times it was at a deserted park. With the extra income, Bruce finally liberated himself from his parents.

Like many enterprising young men, Bruce had in mind to start his first *kwoon* (school) in Seattle and from there spread throughout the United States. "I was getting tired of serving and washing dishes. It is easier to teach kung fu even though I didn't care to do that either," he commented to me.

Bruce was proud of his dialect and he adamantly insisted that "kung" in kung fu should be pronounced "gung" when discussing his school. "The Mandarin or northern Chinese will speak with a 'k' sound but we use the 'g' sound," he explained, "and that's how I spell it too." (In this book, the Americanized spelling of "kung fu" is used.)

By the time Bruce opened his first school, karate was already firmly established in the U.S. The Americans had accepted karate much more quickly than judo or jujitsu. Many ex-servicemen sponsored Japanese and Korean instructors to teach on a full-time basis. Schools sprang up all over the country, especially in California and New York. Championship matches were held, continually drawing as many as 1,000 participants. Some players traveled across the country to compete. Kung fu was in its embryo stage and hardly anyone knew it.

Bruce opened his first Jun Fan Gung-fu School in Seattle's Chinatown, trying to capitalize on the congregated Oriental population. But he soon learned that the sparse Oriental population would limit his enrollment to just a few students, barely enough to pay his rent. Assuming that college students were more interested in his art, he closed his first school and opened another near the campus of the University of Washington.

Unfortunately, the college students weren't flocking to his kwoon as Bruce had anticipated. At that moment he must have felt that he had jumped from the frying pan into the fire as he had to pay higher rent for this more modern and spacious hall. Undismayed, Bruce and his assissant, Taky Kimura, began to educate the public by putting on demonstrations on campus.

It was during one of these demonstrations that Bruce encountered his first altercation. "While explaining the art as the forerunner of karate, I was rudely interrupted by a black belt karate guy from Japan who sat in front of the stage," Bruce related.

" 'No, no karate not from China. Come from Japan!' he hollered."

Bruce reiterated superciliously, "Karate is from kung fu."

After the demonstration and with most of the crowd gone, the nationalistic young Japanese challenged Bruce.

"You want to fight?"

"Anytime," Bruce replied.

"OK. I fight you next week."

Bruce's temper was rising rapidly. "Why not now?" he insisted.

Before a sparse crowd, comprised mostly of Bruce's students and his challenger's friends, both men squared off. Bruce stood in his wing chun stance while the Japanese assumed the karate stance.

The fight was brief. "It only took me two seconds to dispose of him," Bruce related to me. "He was too slow and too stiff."

Bruce never had any doubt about the outcome. Brash, young and full of confidence, he didn't think anyone in the city nor in this new country could beat him. To get into a scrap was inevitable, he felt, because it was a common occurrence in Hong Kong for one style to challenge another to prove which was superior. But he never anticipated that he would be fighting so soon and especially against someone from another type of martial art.

Seattle never became a martial arts city at that time. Maybe it was because the people were too conservative or more likely it was due to the scarcity of Orientals to influence the rest of the public. Anyway, Bruce's dream began to crumble. Students came but never remained long. It was

Bruce as a young man in Seattle.

an uphill battle all the way.

In 1964, James Lee suggested that Bruce come to Oakland. Bruce had only one year left at the University, but decided to quit. He shut the door to his kwoon and instructed his assistant to return to Chinatown to operate a closed school—more like a private club with just a few old students and friends.

Oakland, California is only six miles away from San Francisco if you drive across the San Francisco-Oakland Bay Bridge. The normal temperature fluctuates between 48 degrees in January to 71 degrees in September. Although the adjoining cities are slightly warmer than Seattle, on a cool day the sea breeze can really chill your body—similar to Hong Kong's winter.

San Francisco's Chinatown is like a miniature Hong Kong with its many tiny shops structured after the old country's. For instance, bright red colors are used lavishly on many of its buildings. Signs scrolled in Chinese characters are all over. The whole atmosphere must be beguiling on the first visit. It's difficult to comprehend that you're still in the U.S. and not in some Asian town.

As you walk through the city, the streets are jammed with Chinese. The few whites you might see are probably curious tourists looking for bargains. The spoken language and the shrill music are distinctively exotic. The pungent odor from some of the specialty shops can be nauseating.

Since 1950 the population of both San Francisco and Oakland had been dwindling as upper and middle classes abandoned the city life and moved to the suburbs. By the time Bruce and Jimmy Lee opened their school in Oakland, the urban population was heavily dominated by the poor whites, blacks and a new breed of people—immigrants from Hong Kong.

Many of these new arrivals couldn't speak English. They couldn't cope with school and many began to drop out. Without schooling and not knowing English, they couldn't find jobs. They became the misfits of the Bay area.

As more and more immigrants came, the crime in Chinatown began to swell as young hoodlums formed street gangs. They started to harass merchants and tourists. In the beginning it was purse snatching, but as they became bolder, it was armed robbery and even murder.

Bruce told me that some of these men were formerly Mao Tse-tung's Red Guards. "When Red China was finally under Mao's control, he had no use for the Red Guards," he explained. "Actually, they became a menace to him as they were only trained to carry out his orders to maim or kill. These guys had no feelings at all. They'd shoot a guy in the face as if they were shooting a dog.

"When their service was no longer needed, some of these guys sneaked out to Hong Kong the same way as the other refugees. Somehow a few found a way to get here (San Francisco Chinatown)."

Although the kung fu school in Oakland fared better than Seattle, it only brought in enough income to survive on day-to-day. During that period Bruce and his new bride, Linda, didn't need much as they both lived with

14

Jimmy, his ailing wife and his two kids. Besides, steady income came from Jimmy as he continued to work as a welder while Bruce concentrated on the kwoon.

As Bruce's fame grew, he added more friends and also created more enemies. The kung fu leaders in San Francisco didn't appreciate his non-conformist attitude. For years they had successfully kept the art of kung fu a secret and selected their students with great discretion. They taught no other race but their own.

Bruce, on the other hand, had no intention of carrying on their practice. He taught anyone who was interested and willing to learn. Even in Seattle, his students were a mixture of different races.

One day while Bruce, Linda and Jimmy were at the kwoon cleaning up, a kung fu expert and his students dropped in. Wong J. Man, who recently had arrived from Hong Kong, presented Bruce a written ultimatum to either cease teaching other races or close his school. "That sonovabitch, he thought he could tell me what to do. You know me, I don't take any crap from nobody," Bruce said to me. "That paper had all the names of the *sifu* (instructors) from Chinatown, but they don't scare me."

Scare? Not Bruce. Instead, his blood pressure began to rise. "OK," he said, trying to keep his voice calm, "if you wanna fight, let's get with it!"

Wong J. Man's bluff didn't work. Startled, he tried to buy time by setting a day for the match and tried to outline the rules for it. But Bruce wouldn't go for such nonsense. "Since you're the one who's challenging me, then I'll make the rules. Everything goes and the match is right now."

Jimmy kept the others from interfering as both men faced each other. Bruce stood in his wing chun stance as his opponent got into a horse stance. Confident, Bruce quickly became the aggressor, pressing his opponent who started to back off. As Bruce kept putting on the pressure, Wong began to retreat faster and faster. Finally, he turned and ran with Bruce right on his heels.

"I chased him and, like a fool, kept punching him behind his head and back. Soon my fists began to swell from his hard head," he grinned. "Finally, I did something I'd never done before. I just put my arm around his neck and knocked him on his ass. I kept whacking him (on the floor) until he gave up."

Jimmy told me later that the Chinese community left them alone after that one incident. "You know that guy Bruce beat up, he's an ass. After the fight, he went to the Chinese newspaper in San Francisco and told them that he'd beaten up Bruce," Jimmy explained shaking his head.

The incident in their Oakland kwoon was the turning point in Bruce's way of fighting. If it wasn't for that fight, jeet kune do may never have been created. "It really bugged me after the fight," Bruce said. "It was the first time I felt something wrong with the way I was fighting. The fight took too long and I didn't know what to do when he ran. Getting my fists bruised from punching the sonavabitch's head was kinda stupid. I knew right then, I had to do something (about my fighting)."

Bruce at Lake Washington.

Bruce demonstrates his martial arts prowess while sparring blindfolded at the Long Beach Sports Arena.

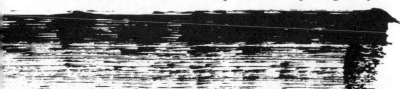

The Challenges

3

When Bruce Lee's fists stopped hurting and even when the battle at Oakland began to fade away, his determination to find a perfect fighting method never abated. Using wing chun kung fu's techniques as his base, he began to slowly develop a simple, but more effective, way of fighting.

In Bruce's dilemma, most martial artists would have probably visited other schools, but not Bruce. Instead, he earnestly delved into any available self-defense books he could get his hands on. He studied and collected books on wrestling, boxing, fencing, judo, karate, jujitsu, etc. He jotted down anything of interest as he went along. Some of the notes were of value to his new style which he later named *jeet kune do*. But much of the information he gathered was never incorporated in his new style.

Bruce had no intention of publishing the notes he had accumulated—they were strictly for his own reference. However, after his death, his compilation was published as a text called *Tao of Jeet Kune Do*.

Bruce always preached that the art of fighting should be simple. But readers of the eclectic *Tao* may find this isn't so as the book is complicated and equivocal. The editor of the book attempted to keep Bruce's notes intact, but his good intentions created an important, but difficult, book.

By the time I met Bruce, he had an extensive library of authentic, as well as trashy, books on the martial arts. He also collected a few books on acting and on Oriental philosophy. Bruce didn't buy the books to exhibit. He actually, when he had time, spent hours perusing the books. He concentrated heavily on the karate books and dissected each technique. Then, he would find a countertechnique as he learned its weakness.

The evening of August 2, 1964, was a memorable one for Bruce. He was invited to perform at Ed Parker's Long Beach International Karate Championships. This tournament was one of the most prestigious, oldest, and largest in the United States. During its heyday, it drew as many as 3,000 contestants from lowly novices to the advanced competitors and as many as 8,000 spectators. Even today, it's still considered an important annual affair to many karate enthusiasts.

Long Beach has always been noted as a progressive and innovative city. Located about 30 miles south of downtown Los Angeles, it is one of the wealthiest cities in Southern California. Its main tourist attractions are the majestic ship, the *Queen Mary*, which has been converted into a hotel/museum, and the world's largest airplane, Howard Hughes' *Spruce Goose*. The many oil wells which augment the city's income considerably are another attraction (or detraction) in Long Beach.

The more than 300,000 citizens don't seem to mind the creaking sound of the horse-shaped, steel derricks which keep pumping oil endlessly. These unsightly structures are spotted throughout the area—even situated in well-kept communities. But the most impressive oil platform is jutting offshore just a few hundred strokes from the Long Beach Sports Arena where the International Karate Championships are held.

To the unwary, they'll never guess it's an oil platform because the structure is cleverly camouflaged as an island. The man-made island even has palms which hide the monstrous steel derricks from the shores.

Bruce at S. Henry Cho's All American Tournament, presenting an award to Chuck Norris.

At night the island has a carnival atmosphere with radiant lights that beam across the water. The lights are so powerful that the whole island illuminates as if purposely built for a movie scene to depict a paradise island.

Bruce used Jimmy Lee and Taky Kimura as his punching partners that August night. It was before the biggest crowd he would be performing for so far. And Bruce gave a stunning exhibition of his rarely seen art. Although Bruce was endowed with a natural showmanship quality he didn't need it that evening to rouse the crowd. His skill was impressive enough that even Tsutomu Ohshima, a high-ranking karate instructor, commented: "When I saw his demonstration, I knew he was highly skillful in his art. For one so young, he's very good."

To awe a martial artist from another style is rare. To receive an accolade from one who studies another art is almost unheard of. Generally, martial artists are very envious of their counterparts and are extremely opinionated. It's almost impossible to convince them that there may be other superior martial arts beside their own.

That one-night performance had boosted Bruce's fame as a top martial artist on the West Coast. It also opened the door, unexpectedly, to Hollywood. In the audience sat a movie producer who was captivated by the young man. A few days later he invited Bruce to a screen test which he successfully passed to become Kato of the *Green Hornet* TV series.

His role as Kato didn't establish him as a serious or promising actor, but it did open the door to the Hollywood circle which was important to any young aspiring actor.

Long before I'd met Bruce I'd heard a rumor that he'd knocked down Frank Sinatra's bodyguard in Las Vegas. Loquacious Bruce normally would relate his experiences to me, but for some unknown reason, he never discussed that incident. In the beginning, I didn't pursue it because I felt that he would eventually tell me about it. But after months had gone by and I had heard just about all his exploits except about Las Vegas, I asked Bruce directly if the story was true.

Bruce looked at me seriously and hesitated for a moment as if to assure himself that he had heard me correctly. Then he reluctantly replied, "It wasn't Frank Sinatra's; it was Vic Damone's (the singer). No, it wasn't his bodyguard; it was the security guard at the casino. There's not much to say. I just let go a side kick to his jaw and the big muthah just dropped. Then I walked out of the place."

Usually Bruce was eager to elaborate his experiences but that was the only time, I can recall, he really cut it brief. He never brought up that incident again. Sometimes, I just wonder if he was at fault.

Nevertheless, that rumor, ironically, brought him in touch with some top Hollywood personalities, such as Steve McQueen and Stirling Silliphant. Actually, it was the late Jay Sebring who first introduced his name to these men. Sebring was the most popular hair stylist in Los Angeles and his clientele included some of the most successful men. Whenever these men came to visit him, he would talk about Bruce's prowess. Silliphant,

the Academy-award-winning screenwriter, happened to be the most zealous of the bunch.

Silliphant soon got hold of Bruce and became his first celebrity student. "For an old man he's pretty good," Bruce used to say, "He's quick with his feet. It proves that a guy who studied fencing (European style) will do good in JKD because of (using) the same footwork."

Bruce, an iconoclast, created many enemies among his peers—especially when he criticized the classical martial arts systems. I remember once a kung fu instructor really got hot when he read one of Bruce's articles in BLACK BELT magazine. The irate instructor called our office and demanded a space in the magazine. ". . . that kid (referring to Bruce) doesn't know what he's talking about," he complained. "Kung fu is an old art and takes a lifetime to know . . . he's too young to really know."

The assistant editor invited the instructor over the following morning for an interview. Then, foolishly, called up Bruce and told him what the instructor had said about him.

Early the next morning, Bruce unexpectedly stopped by my office and I asked him what brought him down so early. "The editor is supposed to talk to this sifu and I'd like to see him," he replied.

"What for?" I asked.

"He said I'm too young and don't know shit about kung fu. I just want to hear it from him."

Exactly at ten o'clock, a middle-aged Chinese man entered the assistant editor's office. Bruce glanced across the room and noticed him there. "Well, I better get this over," Bruce said as he stood up and walked out of my office.

A second later, before the guest could even settle down, I could hear Bruce's voice loud and clear, "Are you the guy who don't like what I said in the magazine?"

Then I heard a soft mumble, "You're Bruce Lee, huh? Yeah, you're too young to know kung fu thoroughly."

Quickly Bruce responded, "You want to play?"

By this time, Bruce's voice was blatant and I could sense the tension in that room.

Then I overheard the kung fu instructor's powerful reply, "Kung fu is not play. It's a serious art and I'll only use (it) in a life-and-death situation."

Unhesitantly Bruce accepted the challenge, "OK, let's go somewhere right now and have it out your way."

I anticipated both men stepping out of the room so I kept my eyes on the door, but nothing happened. No one came out nor did I hear anymore voices.

It must have been ten minutes of silence before I heard the scraping of a chair. Moments later, Bruce appeared. Wearing a smile on his face, he waved his hand and said that he'd see me again and left.

Afterward, the secretary, who had been sitting in the adjoining room, trembled in: "I was so scared. I really thought Bruce was going to hit him. I'm glad he (the kung fu instructor) backed down."

Bruce with actress Sharon Tate.

Coincidentally, a few months later Bruce met the sifu again in a completely different situation. Bruce was selected as the technical director for a movie called *The Wrecking Crew* in which Dean Martin had the leading role. The action-packed movie contained several heavy fighting scenes. It was Bruce's job to hire the extras for those scenes and to direct them.

It seems that whenever the studios wanted martial artists, they didn't have to advertise. Somehow, word got to them quickly. And it was no different when Bruce was trying to find them. Several martial artists showed up like Mike Stone, Chuck Norris, Ed Parker and even the long-haired sifu.

"I told all of them that if they wanna be in the movie, they had to demonstrate their skills," Bruce related to me later. "So I went ahead and did a combination of punches and kicks and told them to do the same.

"When he (the sifu) saw what he had to do—fast triple left and right kicks, plus a low fake with a high hook kick—it musta been too much for him because he didn't even try. He just walked out," Bruce laughed.

I recollect Bruce leaving home early in the morning—around four o'clock—to drive to the location. "They're gonna shoot mostly in the desert," he complained. "I don't like to stay over; prefer going back and forth even if it takes two hours each way. It's a pain in the ass but I can't bitch. They're paying me 11 grand for less than a month's work."

Bruce mentioned that some of the martial artists were real horny around the attractive actresses. "I can't believe what these guys are saying to the girls. Boy, it's embarrassing to me because I'm classified as one of them (a martial artist)."

Bruce's job was to prepare each actor and actress to fight with realism, but he encountered some problems. "I tried to teach Dean Martin how to kick but he was too lazy and too clumsy. We had to use Mike Stone (his stand-in) mostly. Sharon (Tate) and Nancy (Kwan) were better. They were doing side kicks pretty good with just a minimum of teaching. Nancy asked me to teach her privately, but I told her she can't afford me."

Bruce's derogatory remarks on classical kung fu had more repercussion than he even anticipated. One sifu from New York sent his top student to Los Angeles to contend with the maverick. The young man was smart enough to stop by my office first because, in a matter of minutes, Bruce was on his way to meet him. At that time he lived in Culver City which was only four miles away.

I'm accustomed to seeing Bruce greet people with a friendly wide smile but not that time. He entered my office sullenly and after the formal introduction, he asked the kid bluntly, "What can I do for you?"

Set aback by Bruce's brusqueness, the young man stammered, "I . . . I just wanted to see you because I'm also in kung fu."

"What style?"

"Praying mantis," he answered.

Immediately Bruce began to compare techniques. "How do you punch?"

When the lad formed his right fist with the curled middle-finger protruding, Bruce asked him why he did that.

"It's more effective," he responded.

"Hit my stomach with that," Bruce urged.

When the young man reluctantly punched Bruce's muscular abdomen, Bruce just laughed and said, "You can't hurt anyone like that."

Then Bruce copied the fist exactly and said that he would like to repeat the punch on the guy's belly. He jammed his fist into his solar plexus and sneered, "See it's no good. You can't knock down anyone with that punch."

Meanwhile, the guy couldn't respond right away because the impact from Bruce's punch was forceful enough to shake him up—it took him a while to recover from the blow. Bruce could be sadistic at times, but I didn't think he was then. I felt that he was either trying to provoke or scare him.

"I don't like to throw a punch if it's not gonna do any damage," Bruce continued. "When I hit, I wanna make sure my opponent is either knocked off his feet or can't counter right away."

Then he asked the young man to stand up. "I'd like to show you what I mean by that." Placing his fist on his chest, Bruce thrust it slightly. The seemingly innocent nudge hurled the young man forcefully against the wall. If Bruce was trying to scare him, that did it. The youngster refused to participate in any more exchanges of techniques.

Following lunch, Bruce invited the young man to his home. There, he displayed his awesome power and skill in the art of fighting. The visitor marveled at the human machine before him—punching and kicking with precision, speed and power. Afterward, Bruce casually asked him if he wanted to spar.

The young man promptly, but politely, declined. Then he blurted out, "You're so good, you should not teach anyone but the Chinese!"

Bruce looked at him superciliously and laughed, "I'll teach anyone I want to. Nobody tells me who I should teach. Besides, it's a waste to teach the Chinese only. They're too small and weak. Half of them, even with kung fu, don't have a Chinaman's chance to beat the white guys."

Later Bruce's face turned serious and he asked in a calm and firm voice why he came to Los Angeles.

"Just to visit," the kid said with compunction.

Not satisfied, Bruce began to exhort him, "I don't think you just came here for that. I wanna know the real reason. Did your sifu send you here to meet me?"

Finally, the young man admitted that he was sent to challenge Bruce because his instructor resented his criticism of classical kung fu.

The next day Bruce called me and explained that he had a hunch why the kid wanted to see him and that was why he was rough on him. "In Hong Kong it's a common practice for a sifu to send his top man to do his fighting. If his man wins, the sifu and his student get a reputation. If he loses, it hardly affects the sifu because he's not the one who fought."

Although rumors of Bruce's involvement in fighting were numerous, he really didn't get into that many scraps. Most of the stories were fabri-

Bruce and Bob Wall in the famous fight from Enter the Dragon.

cated. The only other fight that others told me about, which Bruce confirmed, happened while *Enter the Dragon* was being shot.

The schedule to finish *Enter the Dragon* was falling behind. The budget for the movie was already expended. Bruce was extremely exhausted. He was working around the clock: acting, directing and planning. He'd already lost 20 pounds but still continued to work steadfastly in the production, very seldom taking any breaks. He knew this movie was extremely important to his career—a step toward worldwide eminence. It was the one chance he'd been seeking all his life.

At this stage, Bruce, more mature, had learned to control his temper. Since becoming a star in the Far East, he had successfully avoided any physical conflicts. "In the beginning I had a helluva time holding back," Bruce used to say. "These muthahs will come up to me shaking their fists and dare me to fight. You know if they did this to me a few years ago, I'd knock them off their asses. But now I can't do it because these sonavabitches will go right to the newspapers, and boast about how they had beaten me, even if I had kicked their butts in. If they get hurt, they'll sue me for sure because they think I got so much money. I can't win either way so I try to keep my cool. But sometimes, I'm tempted to whack 'em."

The pressure from filming began to wear Bruce down. In the beginning he succeeded ignoring one of the extras who had been taunting him for days. He kept harassing Bruce in Chinese in front of the film crew, "You can't really fight, you're only good in acting!"

Finally, Bruce lost his patience one morning and called the troublesome youth to step forward. "The kid must have been in his 20s," said Bob Wall, one of the actors and a karateka himself. "He (the kid) knew what he was doing as he came out fighting. His form was good and his techniques were solid. He really went after Bruce.

"But Bruce took the kid lightly—as if he was just sparring with him. When the kid threw a punch or kick, Bruce would avoid it and then make a comment in Chinese like, 'Hey, your punch is too weak" or "Your punch is too slow. I can easily counter it like this,' and Bruce would slap his opponent's face lightly.

"The kid went all out and became frustrated as Bruce would just play around with him. When the kid didn't give up and Bruce got tired of the nonsense, he threw a side kick, not too hard, but enough to knock him off his feet."

Wall said that the kid had a lot of spirit because even after he was knocked down, he came right up and resumed the attack. "Bruce had to flatten him with a harder kick before he finally quit."

When I mentioned the incident to Bruce later, he pooh-poohed the whole thing. "I knew the kid had no chance with me so I just fooled around. Nobody can lay a hand on me right now. But it's too bad what happened to the kid later."

"What happened?" I asked.

"He got killed the next day," Bruce answered. "I heard that he got stabbed to death."

"Why?" I inquired.

"Hong Kong is a strange place. Not like the U.S. When a guy tries to put you down and you're a hero with the fans, the fans will do most anything. See, when the kid challenged me, he was putting me down in the minds of some fans. They got angry and killed him."

"Do you know who did it?"

"How would I know? I've got no idea who did it. Chances are he got killed by one or several guys who I've never met. It's not uncommon for someone to kill for something small like that."

A volunteer braces for Bruce's punch in a demonstration.

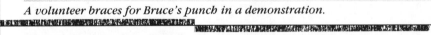

The power in the punch is evident as the volunteer goes flying back.

A Grown-Up Prankster

4

The two masked heros cautiously tiptoed through the corridor, stopping at each door, then straining their ears to the conversation inside. One was dressed in a green suit and hat; the other, a black suit with a chauffer's cap. Finally, the green masquerader seemed to locate the room he was seeking. He tried the doorknob, but it was locked.

He turned his head and looked at the smaller man and nodded. His companion stepped back a couple feet, studied the door and then leapt toward it. With a powerful kick, he broke it in.

Once inside, both men were face-to-face with several hoods. The bigger man used his hands exclusively—punching and pushing—while his companion depended mostly on his deft feet to overpower the hoods.

These two nostalgic heroes, the Green Hornet and Kato, seemed outlandish and puerile to the adult television viewers but, nevertheless, they attracted a large following among the kids, especially those in their early teens. For the first time the kids had a chance to see a skilled practitioner using his feet to kick. Although movies and television had had karate kicks in their stories before, they weren't emphasized as predominately as in the *Green Hornet.*

Bruce Lee's performance as Kato did arouse the public's interest in karate and kung fu but Bruce, himself, didn't receive full recognition as an actor or martial artist. They knew "Kato" better than they knew the actor, Bruce Lee. "Hiding behind the mask," Bruce told me, "didn't help me at all. They really didn't have enough of a chance to see my uncovered face."

Many viewers thought that Bruce had a stand-in or that trick photography was used in the action shots because his kicks were done with complete ease and yet swiftly. The fan magazines and the studio had said that Bruce was a kung fu expert, but his fans were not convinced.

To assure his followers that he was for "real," Bruce decided to perform again at the annual Long Beach (California) International Karate Championships in the summer of 1967. The promoter, Ed Parker, realizing he had a "hot item" as a guest, capitalized on it by promoting Kato extensively in his advertisements. Sure enough, it worked. Over 8,000 spectators came—a record crowd at a karate championship.

Bruce was ebullient when he noticed that many in the crowd were young kids who had dragged their fathers along. Young teens usually didn't attend karate tournaments because they found them boring. Besides, karate meets never seemed to start on time and the delay could annoy everyone. That Sunday night was no different. Actually the tournament opened the day before and by the time the people were seated for that final night, the promoter and his staff had logged almost 48 hours of continuous operation with hardly a break. I recall once, Parker had worked so hard in his tournament that he collapsed from sheer exhaustion.

The preliminary bouts which started an hour late included the lighter-weight fighters who had already defeated several others in the previous grueling day. Now, they were competing for the championships in their divisions. Unlike boxing, even the finals couldn't excite the crowd.

Sometimes karate championships can be very chaotic, especially in an

A young martial artist feels the power of Bruce's punch firsthand.

open tournament like the Long Beach Internationals. Many factions participate and one group may become disenchanted as the competitions continue. After awhile they begin to disrupt the event by vociferously criticizing and condemning the judging or refereeing as bad or unfair. Quite often their underlying motive has racial overtones. And frequently politics do play a part in the final outcome. This kind of disruptive behavior creates disputes that could even develop into a full-scale riot.

Fortunately, at Long Beach the preliminary bouts breezed by without much haggling. A couple hours later the first demonstrations were introduced. Several more took place before Bruce's name was finally announced. Effervescent Bruce quickly stepped up to the microphone and explained what he was planning to do. He opened his demonstration with a one-to-one sparring match against Taky Kimura. A few minutes later he introduced Dan Inosanto and then fought both men simultaneously.

The performance wasn't that outstanding as I could tell by the lukewarm applause from the audience. The effect of Bruce's skill was lost when all the participants wore heavy protective garments and gloves. Even when Bruce landed a direct hit to Inosanto's face, it didn't seem to have enough impact to hurt. However, Inosanto felt otherwise as he complained of a severe headache later on.

The second part of his demonstration was more to the crowd's liking. Bruce asked for volunteers and Bobby Baker of Stockton, California, and a young brown belt came forward. Baker, a six-foot, 200-pound former student of Bruce, was instructed to hold a two-inch punching pad on his chest. Bruce then directed the young man to hit the pad as hard as he could. The brown belt placed his right fist on his hip, focused his concentration on the pad and punched it as hard as he could. The blow caused Baker to take a short step backward.

Next Bruce, grinning, placed a chair about six feet away directly behind Baker. Then Bruce walked up to the microphone and thanked the young volunteer. "Give the young man a hand," he said. "Now I'm gonna hit the pad, too, but only with a one-inch punch."

Bruce moved to the exact spot where the brown belt had stood. To his fans it might have seemed like the re-enactment of the biblical battle between David and Goliath; but this time, David didn't carry a slingshot and Goliath just stood still supporting a pad on his chest.

Bruce slowly, but dramatically, raised his clenched fist near the pad, extending his right arm completely out. With hardly any discernible motion, just a flick of his wrist and a slight twist of his body, he had Baker off his feet and stumbling backward. With hair flying and the pad falling out of his hands, it looked like Baker was clobbered with a baseball bat. He staggered roughly into the awaiting chair. It was Bruce's intent that the force from Baker's weight was supposed to topple the chair, but it didn't work. Instead, the floor was too slippery and the chair carrying Baker just slid about five feet.

The feat was incredible. How could a small man have such power? Even two strong men couldn't have shoved Baker that far back. Bruce's

fans were delighted; they gave him rousing applause this time.

After acknowledging the plaudit, Bruce requested another volunteer from the audience, but nobody responded. Several karate champions' names echoed in the auditorium but none of them wanted any part of it.

After several pleadings, a young man volunteered. He was virtually unknown then but in a few years, he became one of the top contenders in the U.S. Vic Moore, a former boxer and a karate black belt, stood courageously next to Bruce. He had no idea what was in store for him until Bruce announced that he was going to throw a straight punch at Moore's face. "My volunteer only has to block the punch each time."

Bruce then walked several feet away and asked Moore if he was ready. Moore nodded. Bruce swiftly glided toward him and as soon as he was near enough, he threw a straight punch directly at his face, stopping it just before contact. Moore tried a karate block but it was too late, Bruce had already returned his hand. "You missed! Let's do it again but this time, why don't you face the audience on the other side so they can see us," Bruce instructed.

Again Bruce moved about eight paces away and waited for Moore's signal. At his command, Bruce propelled lightly, but swiftly, and shot another straight at Moore's face. Moore again failed to block the punch. "You missed again!" Bruce joshed.

Bruce repeated it six more times and the embarrassed and frustrated Moore could not block one. At the conclusion, the crowd gave Bruce a standing ovation. Proud and elated, Bruce merged into the crowd to accept congratulations from his fans. He finally felt that he had convinced them that he wasn't only an actor, but more importantly, a martial artist.

After Bruce's performance, a crowd began to form by the exit. I thought, at first, it was intermission. But when the emcee announced that there would be no intermission because the program was running an hour behind, I felt that maybe they were taking a break—taking in some fresh air and stretching their legs. After all, they'd been sitting on the hard bleachers for more than three hours.

With over half of the crowd gone, the huge auditorium seemed to turn into a morgue. The stillness and the empty bleachers took away whatever interest I had in the events yet to come. While sitting there with the remaining crowd, somehow, I kept looking at the exit where the mob of people gathered, hoping that most of them would return to their seats, but nobody did. Then, it finally dawned on me that most of the audience came to see Bruce and not the competition. They weren't interested in karate, just in Bruce.

About three months later, I met Bobby Baker at one of Bruce's birthday parties which he gave each year, inviting some of his students who were close to him, martial arts pals, and some movie-star friends. At the party, I asked Baker how he felt from the punch he had received at the demonstration in Long Beach and he answered, "It didn't seem like it was a heavy blow but I told Bruce not to ask for volunteers anymore. It's too risky. He's going to be sued someday.

"After that punch," Baker continued, "I couldn't go to work the next day. My chest hurt so much that I thought something was broken. I was real scared."

When word filtered out that Bruce could pack a crowd in, promoters from other areas began to invite him to their events. At one of Jhoon Rhee's National Karate Championships in Washington, D.C., Bruce was so popular, especially with the kids, he needed protection from the frenzied fans. "We needed a dozens of us black belts to guard him," said Ed Parker, "otherwise, they'd have ripped him apart. I didn't realize how popular he was until then."

Bruce, to a certain extent, was soft-hearted. Generally, he was willing to do favors for people even if he didn't know them. But many times he consented because he couldn't refuse unless he really knew the person. This peccadillo of not being able to say "no" had upset him a few times. Once Bruce accepted an invitation to appear at a karate championship in New York and was treated very shoddily. But he didn't gripe at the promoter directly. Instead, he just quit accepting any more invitations.

"You know karate guys are the only ones who don't pay me a single penny to perform," he complained. "When I was invited to a parade recently, I got paid $4,000. I don't mind helping out the martial artists but since I'm the drawing power and not getting paid, at least, I expect to be treated good. But that guy in New York was too much, he placed me in a second-rate hotel and I had to find my own transportation.

"When I'm sent out by the film producers, they make sure that a limousine is waiting at the airport and always book a first-class hotel; otherwise, the guild (union) gets after them. But that guy (New York promoter) thinks that I'm stupid," he continued. "Wait until he invites me again. From now on I ain't gonna go nowhere for nothing."

The following year the same promoter sent him an invitation, but Bruce just ignored it. Later, I learned that the promoter, even without Bruce's knowledge, went ahead and advertised that Bruce would be his special guest for the tournament. When Bruce didn't show up, the promoter apologized to the audience that his special guest couldn't make it because of another sudden commitment.

The chicanery did succeed because by using Bruce's name, the promoter was able to pack them in. Later, Bruce learned that many other unscrupulous promoters from coast to coast were mulcting the public the same way. "I don't know how to stop them," Bruce complained to me. "These guys don't even take the trouble to send me invitations anymore. They just use my name without my knowledge. I only hear or read about it after the tournament is long over."

Bruce's last public performance was in the Bahamas when Jhoon Rhee, a close friend, invited him over. Bruce never broke bricks or boards in public because he always felt that phase of the art was not important. He emphasized that breaking was strictly for showmanship and anyone could do it because skill was not required. "Breaking a board or brick is not the same as trying to hit your opponent," he said. "Just because you can break

several boards doesn't guarantee that you're going to beat your opponent. *Boards do not hit back.* Yep, I was the guy who first coined that."

I don't know what prompted Bruce to go up on stage and, for the first time, demonstrate some breaking techniques—a complete turnabout. Bruce had seen many karate demonstrations where one or two pine boards were held dangling from a hand. Usually a roundhouse snap kick was used to break them. In the Bahamas he decided to go for more. He always had to surpass anyone or any act. He had a volunteer holding five boards dangling from his extended hand. Bruce knew the challenge before him was not easy; he had never tried it before.

Stepping several feet away he focused completely on the target, then quickly moved in delivering a side kick at the right moment. Three boards broke completely but the other two were left intact. Not satisfied, Bruce replaced the three broken boards and asked the volunteer to hold them again.

On his second time around Bruce kicked the target perfectly but the boards flew out of the volunteer's hands. When the boards were inspected, all five were either broken or cracked. "I don't think the last board broke from my kick," Bruce chuckled. "I think it broke when it hit the ground."

Bruce explained that "to break one or two boards is easy, but to break more than that is not that easy when held loosely. If held solidly, it's no problem, just use a thrust kick. What I had to use was a side kick with snap and thrust. I needed both speed and power. I don't know anyone who has ever used both effectively."

Splinters fly as Bruce shatters a stack of boards with a back kick.

A couple of days after his trip to the Bahamas, Bruce excitedly called me up. "I can now break two-inch boards by dropping them."

"What do you mean?" I asked. "You mean to tell me that you can break a board in mid-air?"

"Yep," he laughed. "I spent all day from morning till late evening to learn it. But now, it comes easy; I can just break almost every board I drop."

Bruce had done breaking techniques prior to then in the privacy of his friends. Once he had Ted Wong and Dan Inosanto holding onto eight pieces of two-inch boards with Steve McQueen bracing both men from the rear. Because the boards were too thick to hold, he had them taped together.

"I split every board with my side kick, some shattered and others cracked completely," he proudly told me.

Confused, I shook my head, not because he had broken 16 inches of board, but for using McQueen. "Aren't you worried that he (McQueen) might get hurt from one of the flying boards or splinters?"

Bruce laughed at me and said, "No, if he gets hurt, it's his own fault, he wanted to do it."

Some people thought Bruce was a big show-off, but to me, I felt that he sometimes acted more puerile than egotistic. Like a kid who had to show his new toy, Bruce had to prove that he had incredible strength. I

remember one night while working out at his Culver City home, a friend brought a guest along to watch. After the workout, Bruce promptly went up to the guest and asked him to hold onto an air-filled shield, an apparatus made of canvas and generally used by football players to practice kicking. The guest, a man in his 30s, politely refused. Bruce asked again but the medium-built man smiled and shook his head.

"C'mon," Bruce badgered, "I'm not gonna kick hard!"

Finally, the man submitted after Bruce's persistence.

Bruce carefully showed him how to hold the apparatus. After he had him ready, he stood back and repeated, "Don't worry, I'm not gonna kick hard." Then, he gestured for one of us to stand behind the jittery man. This was a precaution Bruce always adhered to. When he delivered his kick the force was so powerful that it could hurl the person into the wall. Unless he placed someone to catch him, he might be seriously injured.

But the precaution was for nought this time. When Bruce launched his kick, the man was so frightened that he closed his eyes and turned his body inadvertently. Instead of being hurled back, he fell real hard to the floor, shattering the glass of his expensive wristwatch.

"Hey, you screwed yourself up," Bruce scolded. "Why did you turn your body? That's why you fell down. You should have listened to me, cause my kick wasn't that hard."

At that moment, I thought Bruce would apoligize but he didn't. Actually, he didn't even display any compunction. He just carried on as if nothing had happened.

Many times I used to wonder if Bruce really knew his own strength. On one assignment for BLACK BELT magazine, we visited Bruce to do a photo shoot for an article on his training methods. He had Ted Wong, a close friend and student, standing next to a 75-pound punching bag. Wong was told to use his back to support the heavy bag while Bruce stood in the opposite direction.

As soon as our photographer gave the signal, Bruce moved swiftly toward his target. The next moment, I heard a solid thump. At the same time, I saw Wong being hurled forward roughly from the repercussion of the blow. Bruce and Wong repeated the procedures several times until our photographer was satisfied he had a good shot.

At the conclusion, I felt sorry for Wong who was trying his best to keep himself immobile, but the impact from Bruce's kick was painfully hurling him forward.

When Bruce and Wong came to visit the following day, Wong had a brace around his neck. Surprised, I asked him if he got into an auto accident. He responded negatively and said that he got his whiplash from the bumping he took from the heavy bag.

"Holy mackeral," I whispered to myself, "what if Bruce were to kick someone without the bag between them. Gosh, he could break a guy in two!"

Bruce had no regard as to who his victim would be. When Bruce first met Raymond Chow, the film producer from Hong Kong, in the spring of

1971, he pressured him into holding a shield for him. By that time, Bruce had bought a home in Bel Air, a prestigious neighborhood in the suburbs of Los Angeles.

Although Bruce used his garage as a gym, he always utilized the backyard when it came to kicking the shield. His backyard had ample room and a thick grassy surface to soften anybody's fall.

Chow came to visit Bruce to sign him to a contract to do three movies with him. In his mid-40s at that time, he looked like a typical Asian businessman—well-mannered, unathletic, thick glasses, slim and fragile. I didn't expect Bruce to kick anyone like him. He couldn't be that sadistic. But I was wrong.

"You should have seen his face after I kicked him," Bruce chuckled. "I don't think he ever been so scared in his life. He must have rolled at least four times before he was able to stop 20 feet away. It was funny, his glasses flew one way and he went the other way. Man, was his suit a mess."

But Bruce's most expensive kick occurred while he was teaching Roman Polanski, the noted movie director. Polanski used to take lessons from Bruce intermittently. During one of these sessions at the Los Angeles Athletic Club, Polanski was annoyed at the masseur of the club, who kept repeating after or responding to Bruce's instructions. Whenever Bruce said something, he would repeat it to Polanski or would comment "Yeah, that's how to do it."

When Bruce was about to teach Polanski a kicking technique, Polanski, by now pretty fed up with the masseur's interference, deliberately passed the air shield to him. He ordered him to hold it so he could have a better view of Bruce delivering his kicks.

Bruce at home with his favorte toy—his kicking shield—which he carried everywhere.

In that situation, Bruce must have considered Polanski was too small too catch the big guy, who claimed to be an ex-professional wrestler, so he decided to forego having someone behind him. That meant, only the wall could stop him. "That guy was so big, I felt that I could give a little extra in my kick," Bruce related.

When Bruce kicked, the force lifted the masseur off his feet, almost knocking him right down. But by retaining his footing, the force, instead, drove him hard into the wall. After that jolting experience, the lesson proceeded smoothly and quietly as the masseur dryly watched the men without a word.

But late that night, Bruce had a call from Polanski who frantically explained that he had sent the masseur to the emergency clinic because he complained of a chest pain. "Dammit, I better not kick anybody anymore," Bruce griped later, "that's the most expensive kick I've ever thrown. You know what it costs me—$35 because he had to have an X-ray."

The masseur was lucky because his pain was just temporary. I guess the pain was not caused from hitting the wall but from the shock he had received. But Roger Shimatsu was not as fortunate. Shimatsu, a former managing editor for BLACK BELT, went to see Bruce for an interview on

The Silent Flute, a movie script which was conceived by Bruce.

Late that afternoon, I noticed Shimatsu straggling into the office. His right shoulder dropped like an injured bird with a broken wing. I noticed that he was in severe pain. "What happened to you?" I asked.

"I think my shoulder is dislocated," he winced.

"How did you do that?"

"I held the punching pad for Bruce," he continued, "and he dislocated my shoulder when he swung at it. Gosh, I didn't realize how strong he was. I must have spun three times from that one punch."

Later I discussed the injury with Bruce and he looked puzzled. "I don't understand how he could get hurt. I didn't really hit that hard. Actually, the blow was more of a slap than a punch."

Sometimes, Bruce would slyly lure innocent persons into holding his air shield. Once, while he was flying to Tennessee to teach Steve McQueen, who was on location, Bruce began to chat with a couple of stuntmen who were sitting nearby. Coincidently, they were going to the same place. Flitting from one subject to another, they finally settled on the stuntmen's work. Bruce asked them what the worst kind of physical punishment they have to endure in their work. After consulting with each other, both agreed "a hard body tackle like in football."

Bruce shook his head and disagreed, "I think it's the kick. Being kicked is more shocking than a tackle."

The men rebuffed, adamantly sticking to their conviction.

Getting nowhere, Bruce's lips curled to a sardonic smile. "I guess you guys haven't been really kicked before, huh? I mean a *real* kick! Look, as soon as the plane lands, let me show you."

With that, the argument ceased. Bruce was so eager to convince them that he began to fidget in his seat, looking at his watch every so often. The plane seemed to travel too slow.

When they finally landed, Bruce was the first one out followed closely by the other two. "I headed straight for a service station to put air in my shield. Smart of me to carry it with me that time," he bragged.

If I didn't really know Bruce, I would have thought he lost his marbles. Who in his right mind would come to a strange town and the first thing he does, is play with his grown-up toy just to prove a point.

"After putting in the air," he related to me, "I passed it to the bigger guy."

The stuntman examined the apparatus carefully, trying to find out how to hold it securely. After fumbling with it for a while, ultimately he just wrapped both arms around it, like he was carrying a baby. And Bruce was no help. "Hell, I didn't give a damn how he held it. All I wanted to do was blast him," he said flatly. "The way he carried that thing, if I had misjudged my delivery, I'd have busted his hand. Lucky for him; I kicked perfectly right between his hands."

Then Bruce covered his mouth with his right hand and smirked as if he had a secret to tell me. "You should have seen that guy fly," he gestured with his other hand. "That sonovabitch got hit so hard, he almost went through the service station's big window. One more foot and he'd have gone through.''

The other stuntman stood dumbfoundedly as he watched his friend in a state of shock. Bruce gently picked up his air shield, which dropped when the guy got hit, and offered it to him. But he raised both hands unhesitantly and refused politely.

The big guy, still shaken from the blow, slowly walked toward Bruce, swinging his arms back and forth as if that would take the pain away. ''You should have heard what that guy told me,'' Bruce proudly declared. ''He said he never been hit that hard before. Wanted to know how I got so much power in my kick.''

Bruce throws a punch at a flinching sparring partner.

Bruce was not always successful in duping everyone. When Louis Delgado, one of the top karate fighters in the East Coast, moved to Los Angeles from New York, he anxiously wanted to meet Bruce. But prior to his meeting, Chuck Norris warned Delgado that Bruce liked to show off his power with either his hand or foot.

Sure enough, when both met how true was Norris' account of Bruce's behavior. After a brief exchange of words, Bruce picked up his air shield, wrapped his arms around the handles so the equipment rested on his back, and told Delgado that he wanted to see his kicking technique. Then, he about-faced with the target fully exposed to Delgado.

Delgado just stood still. ''Aren't you gonna kick it?'' Bruce questioned impatiently.

''Nope,'' Delgado replied.

Bruce turned around and faced him, ''Why not?''

Delgado flashed a smile and answered, ''I'll kick it on one condition, if I don't have to hold that thing for you afterward.''

Bruce was taken aback but grinned, ''Who told you?''

''Chuck warned me about you,'' he laughed. ''I heard what you do to all the guys who come up here to see you. I heard how hard your kick is and I don't want any part of it.''

Bruce's eyes twinkled as he turned around and blurted out, ''OK, kick as hard as you can and don't worry, you don't have to hold (the air shield) for me.''

Judo and Jeet Kune Do

5

"Judo is the closest to the real thing," Bruce Lee used to say, "not like karate or aikido. In karate, there's no contact and in aikido, all the attacking is prearranged. Even if you become good in the art, you really don't know whether the technique will work or not in a real situation. I feel sorry for the students who train so hard for so many years, yet question its effectiveness in a real street confrontation."

To Bruce, judo was the most practical of all the martial arts next to jeet kune do (JKD). "Even if judo lacks certain techniques like punching or kicking, at least it has plenty of body contact. When you throw or wrestle a guy down, you know it's working. That's what develops your confidence."

Probably that's why Bruce got along so well with Hayward Nishioka, a former national Amateur Athletic Union (AAU) champion. He would respect Nishioka's opinion more than many other martial artists. Reciprocally, Nishioka was highly impressed with Bruce's prowess and knowledge in the martial arts. Still today, Nishioka praises him lavishly among his peers.

When Bruce was living in Los Angeles, Nishioka would many times bring along a friend to witness this dynamo. Once he brought along Dr. Burt Siedler, a physical education professor at Cal State (Los Angeles). "When he first saw Bruce punching the speed bag," Nishioka smiled, "he (Siedler) mentioned that if Bruce would seriously study boxing, he would be the lightweight champ in a year's time. Then, when he saw Bruce punch the heavy bag and jar it like a heavyweight with lefts and rights, he quickly changed his mind, saying that if Bruce should compete in the ring, he could become a champ in six months.

"Afterward Bruce told me to block his punches," continued Nishioka. "Those punches were so fast that I couldn't block any one of them. When Siedler saw that, he shook his head and changed his mind again, this time telling Bruce that he only needed one month to be the champ."

Another time, Nishioka brought along a student of Shigeru Egami, a noted karate *sensei* (teacher) in Japan. Hashimoto, who was a fourth *dan* (degree) black belt, had never heard of Bruce Lee before. But it didn't take him long to respect Bruce's skills.

Like most martial arts gatherings, their discussions centered around fighting techniques. Hashimoto, a recent arrival, couldn't speak English and had to depend entirely on Nishioka for translation. After several minutes of comparing notes while they leisurely sipped hot tea, Bruce casually asked the skinny visitor if he would like to see his punching technique." When the young man politely consented, Bruce's face instantly glowed, his eyes expressing mischievous intention.

Bruce eagerly picked up his home-made punching pad and quickly passed it to Hashimoto as if he was afraid the foreigner might change his mind. Then Bruce instructed him to hold the pad firmly to his chest. Meanwhile, Nishioka calmly watched the whole proceedings with curiosity. Finally, Bruce raised his right arm high, pulled his long sleeve back over his elbow, lowered his arm until his fist was directly in front of the

pad, barely touching it. Then he flicked his wrist. The seemingly harmless gesture sent the startled karate man crashing into the wall. Nishioka's jaw dropped at this unexpected occurrence before his eyes.

"Hey, Bruce," Nishioka cried, "could you do that to me, too?"

Bruce smiled and nodded, "C'mon."

Nishioka, built much more solidly than Hashimoto, eagerly held the pad to his chest as Bruce prepared to repeat his performance. Nishioka described what followed, "When Bruce punched me, I was almost jolted out of my pants as I bounced off the wall. But I couldn't believe it so I told Bruce to do it again. After the second punch, I was completely convinced. I never thought anyone could be that strong."

That brief display must have awed the fourth dan karateman, too. Earlier he was so determined to exchange notes but after that, he kept mum throughout the rest of the afternoon. On the way home, Nishioka asked his passenger what he thought of Bruce.

"*Osoro-shi-i* (frightening)!" he blurted out. "I never met anybody like him before, not even in Japan."

Nishioka, himself, is not an ordinarly martial artist. For years he dominated the 160-pound division in national judo competitions and finally in 1965, he won the U.S. National Grand Judo Championships, one of the smallest American men to capture it. While in high school, at 17, he was already considered the best judo player in the western United States, out-pointing more mature and experienced players.

In 1960 following his graduation from L.A.'s Roosevelt High School, he was given a scholarship to Tenri University, one of the top judo colleges in Japan. "They (officials of judo) made a big thing of the scholarship, but it was just the transportation cost to Japan," he said. "Once in Japan, I had to find my own way to make a living. In the beginning, I depended heavily upon my parents for support, but later on I took any odd job that was available. To find a job in Japan was hard in the beginning because I didn't speak the language.

"Once I was so broke I went without food for three days. It was the scariest time in my life. Funny in a way, too," he chuckled, "there I was, in a midst of one of the largest cities in the world and I kept thinking to myself, 'what if I should die from starvation!' When you're that young and alone in a strange city, it's awfully frightening. You know the thought of stealing food even crossed my mind. I couldn't help it. I was so weak and hungry from starvation that going to jail at that moment didn't seem so bad—at least, I knew I would be fed and I wouldn't die."

Fortunately, through some martial arts friends, Nishioka finally found steady employment teaching English which paid pretty well. "Many Japanese college kids, especially the graduates, wanted to learn English with the intention of eventually coming to the U.S. Well, I should be thankful because guys like them gave me an opportunity to make a decent living while I was there," he said.

The time Nishioka spent in Japan was far from pleasant. When he first arrived at Tenri University, he was a tough and cocky kid. "I'll never forget the first judo lesson. I thought I was so damn good, I was really sure that I was gonna teach the Japanese some American know-how. On my first day, I expected all eyes to be on me, but you know what? Nobody paid any attention to me. Everyone was busy working out.''

Nishioka finally saw one of the players standing alone. He hurriedly went over and asked with his hands if he'd care to work out. The guy looked at Nishioka agreeably and extended both hands, summoning him to come. "Here's my chance," Nishioka whispered delightfully to himself. "I'll surprise him with a fast throw."

But before Nishioka could get started, he found himself being lifted high in the air and being slammed heavily onto the mat. "I was lucky," Nishioka tried to console himself. "I'll be more cautious from now on." Carefully, he faced his opponent again but "all my skills were no good against him. He was too strong. He threw me over and over again, hardly allowing me time to catch my breath. I felt helpless, outclassed and humiliated. Whatever ego I had was down to zero."

The following day, Nishioka, who was much wiser now, decided to select an easier opponent. He noticed that all the strong players seemed to have cauliflower ears and wore faded and worn-out black belts. He chose a small, thin guy wearing a crisp, new black belt. "I was more humble now," he described himself. "But the second day was almost as bad as the day before. The guy wasn't as tough as the other guy, but he was also too good for me. I was thrown so hard and so many times that all my enthusiasm left me. Until then, I didn't know how it felt to be humiliated.

"But by the end of the following month, I didn't feel humiliated anymore, I was real scared. I was so scared that I dreaded attending classes. Sometimes I even feigned illness to skip training. I even thought of quitting and going back home. I was getting so roughed up that I was afraid I might get seriously hurt or even killed."

After a year at Tenri, which is located in the city of Nara, Nishioka moved to Tokyo to train at the famous Kodokan, the world headquarters for judo. By them, he had overcome his fear and had adapted to their harsh training. He even found time to resume his study of karate with Shigeru Egami. But he only had a mild interest in that particular martial art. His forte was still judo.

The few years studying in Japan paid off. When Nishioka returned to the U.S., he was a formidable threat every time he entered a judo tournament. By 1965 he was one of the best in the country and proved it by winning the national grand championships. That same year he entered his first karate tournament as a brown belt. The tournament was sort of unusual. The contestants were given more freedom than usual in the use of techniques—an advantage to a skilled judo player like Nishioka.

Sure enough, Nishioka who had been placed in the lower-ranked division mowed his opponents down handily with judo sweeps and throws. Meanwhile, in the upper or black belt division, a fourth-dan karateka from France, who flew in to compete, was whipping his opponents.

The final match was unwonted also, pitting a low-ranking karateka

against a high-ranking black belt. But to the spectators it was a special treat. To them, it wasn't a match between two karate competitors, it was judo versus karate.

The rugged Frenchman, considered one of the best in Europe, made his appearance first as he walked to the center of the floor. Confidently, his eyes followed the lowly opponent sauntering after him. After bowing to each other, both men stood in a ready stance, impatiently waiting for the referee's signal of *hajime* (begin). Their waiting was brief as the official seemed eager to see the bout.

At the signal Nishioka abruptly raised his hands high above his head and yelled *"kiai"* like he always did in his judo matches. The piercing sound was to reassure complete confidence in himself, not to scare his opponent.

The haughty Frenchman took the offensive immediately and began to press Nishioka, who kept circling his opponent like a mongoose trying to outwit a cobra. Without warning, the Frenchman, flaunting the rules of the tournament, unleashed a flurry of wild punches catching Nishioka by surprise. He winced as one of the blows hit him solidly on the face. Nishioka glanced quickly at the referee for any forthcoming penalty, and when he saw none, he got furious.

But Nishioka kept his composure and fought with equanimity as the Frenchman, becoming bolder by the minute, pressed him more daringly. However, Nishioka's ploy started to work and, as the Frenchman quickened his pace, he retreated just as fast. The crowd was now silent for they knew their favorite had fallen behind in scoring. Time was also running out.

Then, unexpectedly, Nishioka changed his direction and moved toward his predator, quickly grabbing his *gi* (uniform). Before the Frenchman could counter, he was lifted high off his feet and thrown swiftly to the hard surface. The crowd shrieked as the fragile body met the hard floor. Using his left hand to restrain his fallen foe, Nishioka pumped his right hand and smashed it directly into his eye. He raised his right hand again and just before he could deliver another blow, the referee grabbed his hand and stopped the fight. By now the crowd was tumultuous; it had never seen such a brutal contest before. As the referee consulted with the judges, Nishioka and the Frenchman parted to their respective spots.

Nishioka got a reprisal as he eyed his battered opponent staggering in pain with blood flowing profusely down his face. A few seconds later, the referee walked between both men and acknowledged the winner of the 1965 Nisei Week Karate Championships by directing his hand to Nishioka.

The crowd gave Nishioka rousing applause. They loved every minute of the bloody contest. To Nishioka, though, the bout wasn't that brutal. Actually, he took the contest quite lightly because he knew that judo tournaments are much more risky which he proves with all the operations he's had for shoulder separations, torn knees, etc.

Soon after winning the karate championship, Nishioka was awarded a long overdue black belt from his sensei, Tsutomu Ohshima—the man many have accepted as the "father of American karate." "Hayward (Nishioka) could have been a black belt a long time ago," Ohshima said, "but he didn't put enough time into karate—he likes judo too much."

Satisfied that judo could be effective against karate, Nishioka never competed again in a karate tournament. But he continued to practice the art. After the championships, Nishioka continued to compete in judo tournaments, garnering such awards as the gold medal in the Pan American Games and a fourth-place finish in the 1967 World Judo Championships.

I think Bruce and Nishioka got along because both men respected each other and, to a certain extent, had similar traits. Both of them were mavericks. Nishioka used to harass the judo officials because of their conventional and obsolete methods of running an organization. Bruce infuriated the kung fu instructors by his acrimonious candor in their way of teaching the art. Both men were superior in their respective art. Nishioka, like Bruce, was an iconoclast when it came to the martial arts. His theory is similar: "Why not intermingle the techniques of other arts with mine if they are effective?" This is a complete departure from the traditionalists' concept. But between them, Bruce got the odds as the innovator and fanatic.

In all the years both men knew each other, I don't think they ever worked out together. Their meetings were generally spent exchanging ideas on techniques or Bruce displaying his skills. Their friendship was growing quickly and then Bruce had to leave the country.

Bruce training with his favorite training partner, a wooden dummy.

Developing His Fighting Skills

6

Why was Bruce Lee so good in the fighting scenes of his movies? Was it his know-how of choreography that made him so impressive? Or was it his charisma?

I think both of these played a part in his success, but to those who knew Bruce personally, his biggest asset was his skill in fighting. Bruce could just stand motionless, facing his opponent, and be imposing. I feel that all the training he had behind him was being reflected on the screen.

In his actual sparring, he stalked his opponent like an animal. Face intense, body balanced and relaxed, his piercing eyes would study the opponent's movements. With complete confidence, he would either attack or retreat, depending on his opponent's strategy. He had a repertoire of techniques to baffle anyone. He was as light on his feet as a ballet dancer. His kicks and punches were more powerful than a heavyweight.

To spar against Bruce could be very exasperating. No matter how fast you retreated, he could easily catch you. If you tried to attack, he would be moving backward just enough so you couldn't touch him. Or he would pounce upon you before you could even move. Jhoon Rhee confided in me once "Sparring with Bruce was so frustrating because he would be on you before you could even react. I don't know how he did it but you couldn't beat a guy like him."

Bruce practices wing chun sticky hands with instructor Yip Man.

How did Bruce become so great? Was he born with that talent? Did he have a skilled *sifu* (teacher)?

If you should discuss Bruce's background with his mother, Grace, you would quickly learn that Bruce didn't reveal any athletic inclination as a child. But he must have been very well coordinated to win a cha cha dance contest and also capture Hong Kong's high school boxing championship. What Bruce lacked in physical stature, he more than overcame by using his brains.

Bruce had to be classified as a sort of genius when it came to fighting. He was so obsessed with the martial arts, he tried to learn everything from boxing, wrestling, karate, judo, and other styles of kung fu. He would spend hours reading books on judo, karate, etc., seeking the features and flaws of their techniques. After a while, he got to know the names of all the techniques as well as the countermovements against them.

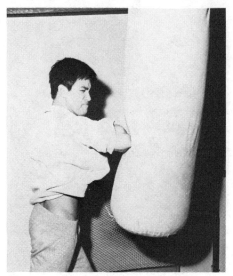

Bruce always emphasized that each workout should be done with the right attitude. Oh yes, he used to kid around in some of our training sessions but when you stood before the heavy or light bag, he expected you to hit it seriously. "If you're not gonna concentrate on delivering your technique, why even attempt to do it? You're just wasting your time and energy. You're better off watching television or goofing off somewhere.

"Remember," he used to point out, "mental concentration is at least 50 percent of your workout. When you punch or kick the heavy bag, you must focus on your target and keep a mental image of kicking or punching through the bag—not at the surface. All your blows must be done with authority and intensity. If you are not giving out 100 percent, then you're not getting the most out of your workout."

Bruce works out with the heavy bag.

Bruce worked constantly to condition his hands.

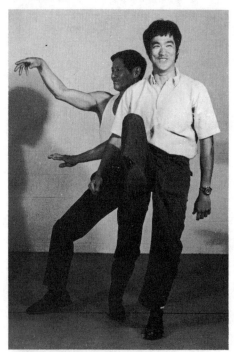
Bruce and student James Yimm Lee clown around at a photo session in preparation for the book Wing Chun Kung Fu.

Someone once asked me if Bruce worked out every moment of the day. I used to joke that he ate and slept jeet kune do. Frankly, Bruce spent a lot of time in the martial arts—not only working out but reading much about them and discussing them with others. Actually, Bruce's scope of interest was quite limited. Besides movies and martial arts, he had no other interests unless they were somehow related or could be applied to the martial arts. These included Oriental philosophies as well as other sports like boxing, weightlifting, etc. But he had no knowledge at all of baseball, football, basketball or other competitive sports.

Even the movies he attended were limited. He concentrated heavily on Chinese kung fu and Japanese *samurai* (sword-fighting) movies. His favorite was the "blind swordsman" series.

Bruce was one of the biggest advocates of sparring. He said, "Without sparring, how do you know if your techniques will work? This is why I don't believe in karate sparring. Karate instructors claim that barefist sparring is the most realistic but I don't think so. When a blow is stopped, really, you won't know if it will knock your opponent on his ass or not. I believe that it's more realistic by wearing gloves and letting go everything you've got. This way, you'll learn to throw your punches with balance, you'll know how powerful your punches are, and to me it just makes sense."

"Wearing gloves and hitting don't give an actual feeling of real fighting," he used to say. "The most realistic is to spar barefists," he explained. "but it's not practical because someone can easily get hurt or killed."

That's why Bruce would buy all kinds of punching equipment—always seeking a material that would feel like human flesh. But even at that, he knew the limitations. "There's no way I can find material that would be exactly like a human body. I'd have to find a hard material like the skull, soft material like the stomach and something in between like the bones."

Bruce thought that finding punching equipment that is closely akin to the human texture was important. "When I hit something with my feet or fist, I like to know how it feels on impact. I like to know how hard I would have to hit to disable an opponent and I also like to know how it would affect my fists. Would I get hurt myself if I hit at a certain angle or way at a certain speed?"

On the wall of his garage hung punching bags filled with sand, beans, and both wood and metal chips. He even had a foam punching pad.

But Bruce thought the most ridiculous martial art was tai chi. "To me, tai chi is really an exercise. It should never be called a part of martial arts because those suckers can't fight. Sure, they'll tell you that they can defend themselves. But when you ask them how can they move fast when they practice their movements so slow, they'll tell you, 'when the real situation arises, I'll be able to move fast.'

"They are telling us that even if they don't punch or kick with speed, when the situation arises, they can do it. If this is true, then the world's top sprinters should just jog in their daily practice. Why don't they do that? Because they are more realistic. In order to be a top sprinter, you have to keep sprinting in your daily practice or you'll never be one. This is true in everything we do: swimming, boxing, skating and even martial arts.''

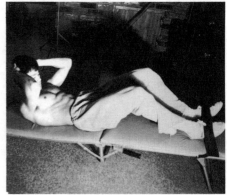

Bruce also believed that no one could achieve peak performance unless he was in good physical condition. ''If you get into the ring and you're not in good condition, how can you last a round? You'll be so fatigued from lack of stamina that by the second or third round, even an inferior opponent will beat you. An out-of-condition athlete, when tired, cannot perform well. Actually, he'd become susceptible to hurt himself, especially in the contact sports. He'd just become careless—a natural tendency when exhausted. You can't throw your punches or kicks properly and you can't even get away from your opponent.''

Bruce believed sit-ups were a must for a martial artist to be in condition.

Bruce also used to poke fun at the ''fat'' instructors. ''Only in the martial arts,'' he sneered, ''can an instructor masquerade as an expert and get away with it. Somehow martial arts instructors can fool their students all the time. Sometimes for years. Either the students are stupid or the instructors are extremely clever.

''When I met someone who raved about a certain instructor as terrific,'' Bruce continued, ''I quickly would ask him why was he good. He usually would say that he knows a lot of techniques, knows his Oriental philosophy and has a good form. So I would counter with 'Have you seen him kick the heavy bag or have you seen him spar?' Majority of the time, the answer would be 'no not really.' ''

Bruce reaffirmed that only in the martial arts, an expert could get away without proving himself. In any other sport the experts must perform. ''Take any sport, if you can't perform, you'll be exposed very quickly. A top swimmer must be able to swim. A marathon runner must be able to run long distances. A high jumper must be able to leap high. But only in the martial arts, an expert does not need to prove that he can fight. All he has to do is have good 'lip service' and know his kata.''

Bruce continued to berate the martial arts instructors because he noticed a great majority of them were so fat—many obese. ''We'd all laugh if a high jumper had a fat body or a real sifu or sensei. Or we'd laugh if a swimmer or a sprinter was built like that. The only athletes who need all the blubber are the guys who do *sumo*,'' he laughed out loud. ''But martial artists need speed and agility and you can't have them unless you're light on your feet.''

Besides stamina, Bruce felt that all martial artists, and matter-of-fact all athletes, should be flexible. He believed that unless your muscles are supple, you couldn't really excel in your endeavor. ''I don't believe that you should kick higher than over your waist in a real situation, but sometimes you have to when the opportunity is there. For instance, if your opponent knows that you can't kick high, he can just concentrate on your punches and low kicks. But if you can spring a kick to his head, you never know how important that kick will be. I'm glad I can kick high because those high kicks are very spectacular in films. The audience loves them.

Stretching was everything to Bruce Lee.

Bruce would condition and harden his hands and fingers by striking hard surfaces.

"Being supple also helps your motion. Your body moves more smoothly—more fluidly. Flexible muscles do not obstruct your movements, while stiff muscles slow you down. Have you noticed the movements of those guys with big, bulky muscles? A martial artists' build should be more like a swimmer. The body should be muscular but smooth. You can't have 'lats' that are so developed that they interfere with your arm movements. I've seen that on some martial artists and they become easy targets on the solar plexus. Their muscles prevent them from covering that area.''

Those who have seen Bruce's performance in movies, quickly notice that his body was muscular but he's also very flexble and fast. Yes, Bruce did work out with weights but he also worked out with other equipment such as the trampoline, several different types of punching bags and an innovative apparatus for stretching made by his students.

Even working on weights, he didn't follow the traditional exercises of a weightlifter or bodybuilder. Bruce made up his own exercises. For instance, to develop his forearms with reverse curls, he added a thick sponge on the bar so his grip would be more difficult. Trying to do a reverse curl with the sponge on the bar made the effort on the forearms twice so strenuous.

Bruce borrowed techniques and movements from different sports and cleverly incorporated them into his style of fighting—jeet kune do. Only a keen and intelligent observer could have accomplished what he did. For instance, he used the stance and movements of a European fencer. Why? Because he noticed that they moved much faster while advancing and retreating than karate or kung fu practitioners. While studying their body movements, he also learned the quick movements of their hands. Eventually, he detected that the fencers were not really that swift but appeared that way because they were not telegraphing their hand movements.

Through trial-and-error, Bruce finally came up with his own stance. Like the European fencer, he stood in an unorthodox stance and he quickly incorporated a non-telegraphic motion when delivering his punches. Bruce had to experiment with this new movement over and over again until he finally mastered it. But Bruce was not just satisfied with new knowledge; he had to go one step further. He had to be much quicker. To do this, he rigged up training equipment which used a long strip of leather that extended vertically from one end to the other. Then he began to finger jab it every day as swiftly as he could. And he supplemented that by punching into the air whenever he thought about it. Soon, he was throwing his punches so rapidly that no one could block them even when they were anticipated.

Bruce was so confident in himself that he began to appear in karate tournaments giving exhibitions. He always asked for volunteers but those who came up were usually not the best martial artists. The champions dared not to come up because they knew that they were no match to Bruce.

As time went by, perfectionist Bruce, never satisfied with his accomplishments, began to do further experimentation. One day he got one of his students to stand before him to block his punch. Instead of just non-telegraphy, he began to throw his punch with a mental image. He concentrated deeply on two spots—his fist and his target—and tried to be oblivious to the rest of his body. It worked. His punches were now so swift that even if a guy tried to anticipate his punch, he couldn't block it.

Most people would be satisfied with what he had accomplished but not Bruce. When he saw that his students were trying to anticipate his movement, he started experimenting with something he had learned from boxing books. He introduced a technique called "broken" rhythm. Instead of just throwing his punches like anyone else, he began to change the tempo. Pretty soon he mastered this movement and he did it so smoothly that an observer couldn't notice it. But when others did it, they looked very awkward.

Bruce practicing his punch.

Bruce Lee's classic fighting stance.

The Fighting Mind

Many people, even today, think that Bruce Lee was only interested in promoting himself and jeet kune do. They felt he was not concerned about the other martial arts. How wrong they were. Surprisingly, Bruce was a proud person and he continued to criticize others if he felt they could improve themselves.

First of all, Bruce was proud of his heritage and always tried to defend the Asian customs and traditions. It irked him when he saw the Oriental martial arts not being taught in a practical way. He tried to expose the flaws in the martial arts, but instead of receiving commendation, he received more antagonism.

The fault was also Bruce's. He bluntly attacked the traditionalists without any reservation. His iconoclastic attitude was too much for some devotees to stomach. Bruce was not hesitant to attack any techniques he felt were useless. For instance, he said that if someone were to choke you from the front, the typical self-defense was to free yourself from the grasp and then poke your fingers in the attacker's eyes or kick his groin. Bruce's solution was to kick him in the groin or poke him in the eyes first. "Why waste your time breaking his hold?" he said.

I think Bruce's critiques and teaching were accepted more by novices than by the experts. However, this didn't deter Bruce. He knew what he was up against and he also knew that many instructors would not listen to him because of his youth. They still carried the old belief that "a young man's knowledge is limited until he has had years of training."

When Bruce learned that he couldn't preach directly to the devotees, he decided to explain his thoughts through BLACK BELT magazine. Bruce succeeded to a degree in reaching more people with his article entitled "Liberate Yourself from Classical Karate," in the September, 1971, issue of BLACK BELT. Bruce emphasized in the beginning of the article that "I seek neither your approval nor to influence you toward my way of thinking. I will be more satisified if . . . you begin to investigate everything for yourself and cease to uncritically accept prescribed formulas that dictate . . ."

To Bruce, "fighting is simple and total." He felt that all the different styles of fighting were unnecessary and "kept men apart from each other rather than unite them."

Bruce used to say to me, "Style screws a guy up because he thinks he has to throw his punches and kicks at an exact path and rhythm. There's no tested or practical theory behind the delivery. Just because someone, centuries ago, said that this is how it should be done, may not necessarily be the best way. A style should never be considered gospel truth, the laws and principles of which can never be violated."

Bruce used to laugh when some martial artists pointed at his feet as he moved with his heels lifted. "That's wrong," they used to criticize, "no power in your blows." Bruce knew that a boxer goes flatfooted when he wants to land heavier blows but he also understood that he moves faster on his insteps. Bruce had proven many times that a punch need not be thrust from your hips to be effective. He believed that a punch can be

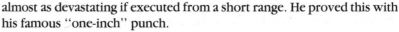

almost as devastating if executed from a short range. He proved this with his famous "one-inch" punch.

Bruce mentioned that too many martial artists used style as a "crutch which limits or blocks the total growth of a martial artist." Day-in and day-out repetitious drills, according to him, would develop some kind of security by the routine, but might also become an impediment.

One of the practices by traditional martial artists that may be a hindrance is the *kata* (prearranged forms). "Anyone who places so much time on kata is wasting his time," Bruce concluded. "How can you do 100 movements in an exact sequence and use them in the streets? Nobody fights the same way. Some grab to wrestle you down. Some punch and some kick."

Bruce explaining a technique at a demonstration.

Paradoxically a martial artist may debilitate himself by studying kata too well, according to Bruce. "I wouldn't be surprised at all if a kata man got whipped by someone who doesn't know how to fight. I think a kata stylist would do better against a skilled fighter. Why? A skilled practitioner of kata can apply his techniques better against someone who also uses the same techniques. But against some bum who doesn't know anything, he would have a problem with his irrational attacks and movements."

Being a nonclassical martial artist, Bruce believed that any art, including fighting, must continue to evolve. "We can't keep still and adhere to an art that existed centuries ago without improving on it. We must not add on more to the arts but must now shed some of the patterns. Like a sculptor, we must eliminate those movements that are not necessary nor effective."

Bruce told us over and over that most of us are so entrenched in the classical teaching that only by liberating ourselves from a style, could we improve quickly. "Everybody has to think for himself," he emphasized. "There's no right way or wrong way in fighting. A right way for a big man may not be a right way for a small man. A right way for someone who is slow may not be a right way for someone who is quick. Each person must understand his weaknesses and his strengths."

Would there be another Bruce Lee in time? Many who knew him well, doubt there will ever be another. But who knows? Great men come and go. If another Bruce Lee shows up, he must be diligent. Bruce claimed he was lazy, and many agreed with him because he didn't like to work for someone Monday through Friday, eight hours a day.

To me, Bruce was far from being lazy. Actually, he was an overzealous perfectionist in what interested him most—martial arts and acting. Although he was an impatient person, he had much perseverance when it involved the martial arts. He could spend hours doing the same technique over and over again until he was satisfied. Fatigue? I don't think he knew the meaning of the word.

A future Bruce Lee must also be a superb athlete. Bruce knew that to be a top martial artist, you must be able to perform more than athletes in other sports. He must have flexibility, strength, quickness and the use of

his body to wrestle, punch and kick. He must be in top physical condition at all times.

Bruce followed a daily ritual. Since he didn't hold a steady job, he had plenty of time to exercise. This usually consisted of running several miles on hilly terrain, working out with weights, and kicking and punching a dummy apparatus built by his students. Everything Bruce indulged in had to be almost perfect. For instance, he would spend hours doing a rapid side kick until his motion was smooth and almost a blur. Even if his knees were hurting, he wouldn't quit. As a consequence, his knees always made a clicking sound when he whipped his foot out.

A dapper Bruce throws a playful punch during a meeting.

Any future Bruce Lee must also be a scholar. Bruce might have been a poor student, but he was an avid reader, especially in philosophy. He tried to apply whatever he had learned from books to his daily life. I feel this adherence to books and their application to life isolated Bruce from we ordinary mortals. While most of us can easily be content with our small accomplishments, Bruce never seemed to be fulfilled. This insatiable thirst for success eventually brought him all the fame and wealth his profession offered.

The next Bruce Lee would also have to have a creative and analytical mind. Bruce was never pleased with any of the martial arts. He was constantly finding faults. He would read a martial arts book and soon be noting the weaknesses in its techniques and how to improve them. He would also find a countermovement for each defense or attack.

One tournament champion realized Bruce's talent and used him to analyze his opponent. Sure enough, each time he entered the ring, he easily outpointed his opponent with just one counterpunch. "This is what's wrong with karate," Bruce remarked. "How can a guy be a winner with just one punch? And see what I meant when I said that karate fighters are almost all stereotyped. You can just about predict each strategy because they all train the same way with almost the same techniques."

Bruce related almost everything in life to the martial arts. He even carried on the philosophy to his acting. It seemed like his mind was on the martial arts 24 hours a day. Although Bruce mentioned that he had a peak just before he left for Hong Kong, I don't think he really did. Because his brain was always creating, I doubt that his fighting skills would have ceased.

He was the type of person who had to find an answer if there was a flaw. Even if there wasn't a flaw, but if the technique was not quite perfect to him, he would attempt to improve on it even if it took him days to do so. Because his techniques were constantly improving and transforming, his students quickly found themselves left far behind if they didn't train with him.

The last few years before his death, Bruce did admit that he should never have coined the words *jeet kune do*, because even then his fighting method was being classified as a style. I don't think Bruce really felt that he had accomplished his aim with the martial arts community.

Bruce Lee always preferred his sparring opponents to wear protective gear so he could go "full-out."

Bruce Didn't Like Bullies

8

He flaunted his opponent, propelling rights and lefts at him. Sweat began to form on Bruce Lee's muscular bare back as he kept forcing the action. His opponent kept backpedaling and held his heavy gloves to his face, trying to protect it from the stinging blows. Bruce played with his opponent like a cat with a trapped mouse.

Suddenly, his opponent delivered a right hook that caught Bruce directly on the jaw. "That's the only mistake I made with Bruce," Dan Lee, a former amateur boxer, said. "After that punch, Bruce got furious and began to pound me. He never let up until he was completely exhausted. I learned not to do that again."

This was Bruce Lee, a hard competitor. He had to show who was the "best" when it came to fighting. But ironically, he never could stand a bully beating up another student. "If I ever caught one of my stronger students beating up on a new inexperienced student in a sparring match," Bruce related, "I'd quickly stop the match and take the young guy's place. When I did, the bully had better be prepared because I'll go all out to beat the hell out of him. But I would only do that to teach him a lesson. To let him know how it feels to be on the other side."

Bruce did not demand respect from his students but, nevertheless, he got it. Although he believed that students should respect their teachers, he didn't demand it. He didn't expect the students to bow or meet him with a kung fu salutation. Actually, after he had introduced JKD, he was gradually moving away from such formality. His new students still addressed him as "sifu," but others, like Ted Wong, called him by his first name.

Maybe, it's because he was still a young man and he, himself, was never introduced to the rigid formality while studying under his sifu, Yip Man, in Hong Kong. "I have to give the Japanese credit for emphasizing rigid formality in their schools," Bruce once said. "When I was taking kung fu, Yip Man never got any kind of respect from his students. He was never able to keep order during our training session. Students used to address him as 'Hey old man!' and even cussed at him if things didn't go their way. I think they respected him less than the man on the street."

When I first met Bruce in 1967, he still had his school in Los Angeles' Chinatown, but he was already losing interest in teaching. Since the *Green Hornet* series had already been canceled, Bruce began to teach lessons privately to Hollywood celebrities. "After *Green Hornet*, I didn't know what I was gonna do," Bruce once commented, "I'm not the type of guy who can sit in an office eight hours a day doing the same routine day-in and day-out. I have to do something different each day and it has to be creative and interesting."

One day Bruce stopped by to see William Dozier, the producer of *Green Hornet*. "When Dozier learned that I wasn't doing anything in the acting field (after the *Green Hornet* series), he suggested that I use my talent and teach celebrities jeet kune do. But when I told him I don't care to teach, he looked at me surprised and asked 'for good money?'

"I wanted to know if I could charge as much as $25 an hour and he said, '$25 an hour is too little. These guys got money to burn and if you don't

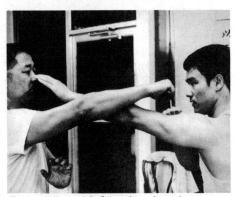

Bruce spars with friend and student Dan Lee.

take it, they'll spend it somewhere else. If I were you, I'd charge them $500 for ten hours of lessons!' ''

For several years this was Bruce's principal income but he also earned some money from the residuals from the *Green Hornet* and cameo parts he played in some other films.

As his income from teaching celebrities began to grow, he seemed to have lost some interest in his school in Chinatown. His visits to his school became so infrequent that some of the new students never had a chance to study under him.

By that time, Bruce felt that jeet kune do was not for everyone and decided to curtail memberships. "I don't want too many in my organization," he said. "The fewer students I have and the harder it is for anyone to join will give my club more prestige and importance. Like anything else, if it's too popular and too easy to join, people won't think too highly of it. Besides, I don't want some of my students to go out and teach the public and make money on JKD—especially if they use my name to draw the students."

Bruce with his students.

Bruce explains a technique to student Dan Inosanto.

When Bruce closed his Chinatown school, his assisant Dan Inosanto continued to teach a handful of the students at his home in Carson, California. Meanwhile Bruce maintained his private lessons with celebrities and also held special sessions with his friends at his home.

Every Wednesday night Ted Wong, Herb Jackson, Bruce and myself converged in Bruce's kitchen at his Culver City home. Bruce lived at that time in one of those ranch-style houses with a high ceiling in the kitchen. The room was so huge that he converted half of it into a gym. It was spacious enough to hang his speed bag, heavy bag and other equipment, but too small to spar in. This we did in his backyard.

His rented house was easy to locate as it was surrounded by a wooden fence and at the entrance stood an ancient black light pole which was always illuminated when he expected company for the evening.

His guests were usually greeted by his friendly Great Dane, Bobo—a clumsy 150-pound dog who would knock down anything in its way, chairs, lamps and even Bruce's four-year-old son. Bobo was especially taken to guests. One day Tony De Leonardis, a former editor of BLACK BELT magazine, went to see Bruce and Bobo wouldn't leave him alone. "That damn dog followed me everywhere. I was so scared I tried to keep Bruce in between us, but he thought it was so funny. He never even made an attempt to put the dog out." After his first visit, De Leonardis never went back.

I particularly didn't care for the dog because he got his saliva all over my pants. Neither Bruce or Linda could control him. He never listened to either one. It was amusing to watch Linda walking the dog, because as soon as the dog began to run, Linda couldn't handle him. "That dog walks me, I don't walk him," Linda smiled. "We even had him at a training school and he's the only dog I know that ever flunked out."

Many times I used to wonder if Bruce used his students just for his convenience, as Herb Jackson sometimes referred to himself as the "chief kicking dummy." I don't think Bruce intentionally tried to use his students, but outsiders might have thought so. He never charged any of us for the lessons but he also got Jackson and James Lee to construct most of the custom-made equipment in his garage. No matter what outsiders thought of Bruce Lee, his students had the utmost loyalty to him. They would do anything for him. None of them ever bad-mouthed him.

Our Wednesday classes began with no formalities—Bruce called us by our first names and we did the same. No bowing and plenty of kidding around. Bruce seemed to enjoy the informal gatherings. He never took anything serious during those classes. One night he had Jackson hold on to a custom-made shield. The shield was made of a spongy material but the backing was of hardwood. When Bruce kicked the shield, the impact was so powerful that the apparatus hit Jackson's face, causing a cut above his eye. Without any remorse Bruce called Linda in to take him to UCLA Medical Center. An hour or so later, Jackson returned with a bandage over his injury. "It wasn't too bad," he forced a smile, "it was just five stitches."

Bruce practices wing chun sticky hands blindfolded with Dan Lee.

Bruce also had keen ears. One day while working out, Ted Wong blurted out Bruce's name. Before Wong could say another word, Bruce stopped him and asked him to repeat his name. When Wong said it again, Bruce suddenly laughed and shouted, "I rike to order flied lice!" I guess the joke was on Bruce as much as on us. We had known Wong for years and saw him every week but nobody detected that he was calling Bruce, "Bluce" all that time. Bruce tried to teach him to pronounce the "r" but to no avail. But then, when Wong used to teach me to use the correct pronunciation of Chinese words, I couldn't do it either.

Before I met Bruce I was into aikido and my main interest was in the development of *ki* (internal strength). Bruce objected to anyone using the words *ki* or *chi*. "The practitioners of kung fu and Japanese martial arts keep using those words to create some kind of magic or mystery to the arts," he said, "when it's only another form of energy. I prefer to use 'flowing energy' or sometimes I'll use 'inner energy.' There's no mystical power about it."

When I learned that Bruce's art was using the same energy as aikido, I was eager to learn especially the sticking-hand exercise *(chi sao)*. Bruce also wanted to practice this form of wing chun exercise to develop his energy further with someone who had the knowledge of it.

Bruce's way of training was overpowering. When he tired me out, he would then pick on Ted Wong. Bruce would never quit until we did. He enjoyed seeing both Wong and myself giving up.

One night I asked Bruce if he taught his students chi sao, applying the flowing energy. He shook his head negatively and said, "Too much trouble to teach them. I've learned it on my own so why can't they? If they don't know, that's their problem."

Even though Dan Inosanto was Bruce's chief instructor, I still think Bruce considered Ted Wong as his protege before his death. Wong was his constant companion for the last few years. Besides working out on

The California beach was the sparring ring for Bruce and student Ted Wong.

A lightning-quick backfist slips past Wong's defenses.

Wednesday nights, Wong also came to see Bruce on weekends. When Bruce needed a sparring partner, it was Wong he selected. But Inosanto ran his club. A physical education instructor, who also taught kempo karate for many years, Inosanto was more capable of running the classes. Bruce also used Inosanto's help in his movies because of his karate experience. It was Inosanto who taught Bruce the use of the nunchaku and the staff in his movies. Bruce was never a weapons man; he only studied those weapons so he could incorporate them into his movies. "A movie becomes boring unless it has variety. By using different weapons, the film becomes more exciting. But it must be done right, or the audience can see the flaws," he once said.

After Bruce's death, both Inosanto and Wong kept their solemn oath and never openly taught jeet kune do to the public. Inosanto still teaches the art but with the emphasis on *escrima*, a Filipino art, and Wong only works out with his friends.

Bruce poses with Ted Wong, left, and Dan Inosanto, right.

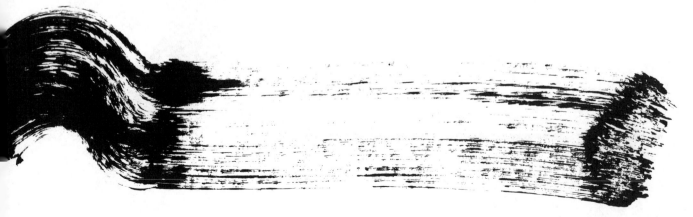

Some Champions Detested Him

9

Bruce was not liked by everyone. There were many martial artists who detested him—even those who claimed or pretended to be his friends. Bruce was not the easiest guy to get along with. He was a proud and intense martial artist and whenever he confronted another competitor, he would unintentionally "test" him. Bruce wasn't rude nor unfriendly. He was so proud of his skill that he just wanted to prove to everyone his superiority (in fighting). Whenever he impressed another—a layman or a martial artist—he would become so excited and obsessed that he'd forget his own strength. In the process, he deflated many a proud champion's ego and may even have physically hurt a few who preferred to suppress their pain.

In all the years I knew Bruce, not once did I see anyone surpass his skill in fighting. He had both speed and power in his hands and feet. There are others like Koichi Tohei with more powerful *ki* (flowing energy), but Bruce was, in my opinion the almost perfect fighting machine. One top competitor told me, with some animosity, that Bruce "has to be the best in everything he attempts. If someone ever beat him, Bruce couldn't take it and would go into a rage."

Jhoon Rhee throws a high kick at Bruce in a seaside sparring match.

Those who could stand Bruce's attitude, and not become humiliated by his superior ability, benefited by his teaching. I don't think Bruce really intended to humiliate or hurt anyone. He sometimes acted like a kid and wanted to show others his skills and their inadequacies. Bruce enjoyed revealing the flaws and weaknesses in the other arts, which he knew by heart—karate, aikido, judo, etc. Many times his overly enthusiastic approach hurt other martial artists' feelings.

Those who seemed to be offended the most were the champions. They, themselves a very proud group, felt they too were good and skillful and when Bruce began to "break apart" their techniques, they became quiet and resentful. They had put in many hours of hard work and couldn't see themselves being upstaged by Bruce, especially if they were in the arts longer than he.

Some were awed by Bruce's skill and returned to learn more, but many didn't come back because they didn't want to be classified as a student of Bruce Lee. Their ego wouldn't allow that. And those who returned would always refer to their meeting as a workout. But those who knew Bruce would chuckle at such a comment because it would be 90 percent output by Bruce and seldom more than ten percent from the others.

Although Bruce had taught several top martial artists intermittently, many didn't want their names to be associated with his. They don't mind if they were referred to as equal in skill, but never inferior. "These guys, just because they're designated as 'champions,' don't want to be classified as my students," Bruce explained. "They want to learn from me but want others to feel that they are equal or almost equal to me. And they want me to say that they are working out with me. To me, working out is for them to contribute also but they don't; it's all one-sided. I have to teach them and that's not working out."

Some of the martial artists felt that Bruce was trying to use their names to enhance his reputation. But Bruce felt otherwise. With a "chip on his

Bruce and Chuck Norris.

shoulder," he'd smile and say, "I know I'm good and that's that!"

Bruce would often get infuriated when someone boasted that they taught Bruce Lee. There were many that claimed that but I don't know of anyone saying it to his face. No one dared to because Bruce would quickly dispel it with a challenge to spar or fight.

Those martial artists who never had to compete for status had a more beneficial relationship with Bruce. Jhoon Rhee, for one, did get along with Bruce very well. Rhee was always eager to know celebrities because he had learned a long time ago that in this country, it pays to know the right people. Since coming to the United States from Korea, Rhee became one of the most successful martial arts entrepreneuers. His organization is one of the largest and most profitable in the country and his students include celebrities in show business, government, business and sports circles. Rhee, himself, is somewhat of a dignitary. He has written several martial arts books, starred in a martial arts movie, appeared on national television, and has been featured in highly circulated national magazines.

Bruce and Rhee got along because their personalities didn't clash. Bruce was boisterous, energetic and a joker. Rhee is a diplomat, reserved and good-natured.

Of all the martial arts instructors and promoters, Rhee was one of the very few who kept his word and took care of Bruce. When Bruce attended his National Karate Championships in Washington, D.C., during the 60s, Rhee's hospitality was great. Rhee was so pleased with the heavy turnout because of the special guest appearance, he later generously offered Bruce and his wife an all-expense-paid vacation to Bermuda.

Although Rhee knew Bruce was the best fighter he had ever seen, he never publicly mentioned it until after Bruce's death. "Bruce's style is great but it can't be taught in a school," he said to me one day. "Everything is so individualized and not too many students can afford private lessons."

Bruce was generous in helping out people whether they were good friends or only acquaintances. I never heard him refuse anyone when being asked for favors. When Rhee wanted to act in a movie, Bruce used his influence with Raymond Chow of Golden Harvest and Rhee got a starring role in a Chinese movie. "I guess every martial artist's wish is to be in a movie," Bruce laughed out loud.

But Bruce was not strictly an altruist. When he formed his own company, Concord, with Raymond Chow and produced the first movie, *Return of the Dragon*, he hired Chuck Norris to be in it. Bruce wasn't concerned about Norris' acting ability, he was more interested in his talent as a fighter and his reputation as a karate champion. "The Chinese audience is still naive," he explained, "and when Norris is presented to them as a karate champ, they'll believe it."

I think Bruce utilized Norris because he could create the fighting scene with more realism. Also, beating Norris in a fight, even staged, would enhance his reputation as a the better fighter in the minds of the Chinese fans. Besides, a battle between Bruce and the world champion makes for good advertising.

Norris, who was seeking to become an actor, saw an opportunity he couldn't pass up. Undeniably, *Return of the Dragon* did eventually open many doors to other films.

Bruce attempted to create movies apart from the cheap, stereotyped flicks produced in Hong Kong. He didn't want his movies to be categorized as "when you see one, you've seen them all" types. So when Kareem Abdul Jabbar vacationed in Hong Kong, Bruce's face lighted up as he quickly perceived the possibility of staging a battle of the century between Jabbar and himself. "When Big Lou walked in the studio, I already had in my mind to be sure to use him in my next film. With me fighting a guy this size, the Chinese fans would eat it up. It will be something they've never seen before. I can already picture the fans' reaction when I do a side kick straight up to his face. This may be the only movie they'll ever see a guy over seven-feet tall fighting someone five-foot-seven," he said, excitedly, with eyes sparkling.

Bruce got along best with those who had no direct competition with him but had similar interests. Hayward Nishioka, former National AAU judo champ, is a black belt in karate but his forte has always been in judo which Bruce showed no interest in. Nishioka, like Bruce, has always been the skeptical type. Although he has studied judo since he was a child, he never stuck to that art alone, like the traditional martial artists. His curious mind led him into other arts, even the sport of amateur wrestling. He did not hesitate to stick his neck out for a cause he believed in, even if he knew the consequence would be grave. That is why he has been at odds with the officials of the national and judo organizations for years—fighting for the rights of players.

Wally Jay of Alameda, California, got along with Bruce because their ideas were similar. Jay, whose arts are jujitsu and judo, liked to experiment between the arts. He borrowed jujitsu techniques and used them in judo, developing more effective techniques in judo competition for his students. His pupils could attest to this since they have been garnering the judo trophies for years. But the national judo organization didn't particularly care for its members to practice other arts. It attempted futilely for Jay to disassociate himself with the art of jujitsu. And Jay's stubborness may have lost him several promotions.

Bruce was widely known to the other martial artists, but he never went out of his way to meet them. Most of them came to see him. Bruce was hospitable by nature and used to invite them all the time to his home. At one time or another several top karate instructors stopped by including Chuck Norris, Bob Wall, Mike Stone, Joe Lewis, etc. But none of them could be considered a student of Bruce because they didn't stay with him long enough—except for Dan Inosanto.

Of all the top competitors in karate, Joe Lewis got the most out of Bruce's expertise. For a few months Lewis spent almost every day at

Bruce corrects the position of Ted Wong's hand while another student listens.

Bruce and Dan Inosanto.

Bruce takes time out from his oceanside battle with Jhoon Rhee to mug for the camera.

Bruce's home, acquiring the finer skills in tournament strategy and technique. Bruce used to even sit in at tournaments and coach Lewis from ringside. Under Bruce's guidance he was almost unbeatable.

Bruce was hospitable but not gullible. One day the head of a large tae kwon do organization offered Bruce a fifth dan as a gesture of friendship, but Bruce politely refused it. "I don't know what that guy's intentions were," Bruce said. "He wanted to use me to elevate himself and sell more of his books. If I accepted the rank, he would have claimed, in his book, that I'm one of his students."

Bruce didn't receive many praises from top martial artists until after his death. I think many were envious of him because he was so good. Besides, Bruce was not modest about showing off his ability and he didn't hesitate to back up his claim against anyone. But, he wasn't truculent; he didn't look for trouble.

When Hayward Nishioka, the former Amateur Athletic Union (AAU) judo champ and a black belt karateman, praised him, Bruce was extremely elated. He explained to me that Nishioka once admitted "he thinks he could beat any of the karate champs in a streetfight, but not against me. I felt that's the highest compliment I can get, especially from a top martial artist like Hayward.

"But you know what?" Bruce continued, "I wouldn't have a chance against a good judoman like him if we were to fight on the ground. Yeah, if there's any flaw in my technique, it's my floor work, but I'll tell you something, nobody is gonna put me down," he pointed out. "Besides, no matter how good you are on the floor, you can't fight more than one guy at a time. I don't care how good you are, you have no chance against two or more people when your mobility is restricted."

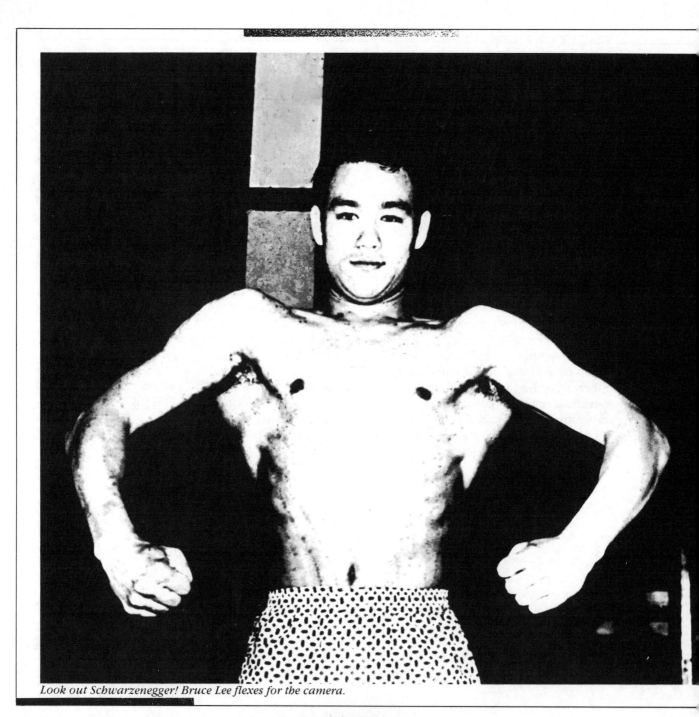

Look out Schwarzenegger! Bruce Lee flexes for the camera.

Muscles Like Steel

10

Perspiration flowed from his forehead and his worn-and-torn sweat-suit was extremely damp. Bruce Lee always seemed to be wet. Even in an air-conditioned room, as soon as he gesticulated, he would quickly perspire.

I remember one night when he rode his exercycle during a workout, he pumped for 45 minutes without stopping. When he got through, he was completely drenched. Even the floor beneath him was so wet that it had to be mopped right away.

Bruce never bragged about his muscular body but he was proud of it, especially of his highly developed abdominal muscles. Many misconstrued that whenever he took his shirt off at a friendly gathering, he was displaying his physique. Probably he was, but I think he took it off more for comfort because I never saw him do that on a cold day.

When Bruce wore loose clothing, he looked like a normally built guy. But underneath the clothing, he was a man with extraordinary muscles. "I've seen many muscular bodybuilders," one of his fans said, "but never like Bruce. He is built perfectly, not bulky. He has muscles on top of muscles. He moves with the finesse of a ballet dancer. Those men with bulky muscles can't move like that, they are too tight and clumsy."

Fred Weintraub, the producer of *Enter the Dragon*, gave this description of Bruce. "Although Bruce lost a lot of weight from overwork at the time we were shooting the movie in Hong Kong, his body never had an inch of fat, it was pure muscles like steel."

Bruce had to work hard to develop those muscles. "I used to have a big, soft belly like the aikido men," he explained to me one day, "because in wing chun (kung fu), like aikido, we were taught to concentrate heavily on our stomach as we practiced *chi sao* (sticking hand technique). I was told to place my feet together, concentrate on the center of my belly, relax and sink my body downward by bending my knees slightly.

We, including my teacher, thought this was the only way to develop flowing energy. The bigger the belly, the stronger the energy. That was the concept then.

"Eventually my stomach protruded and I looked terrible for a young guy. One day I decided to streamline my waist as my thinking began to change. 'How can my strength be dependent upon a big belly, anyway?' It just didn't make sense."

From that revelation, Bruce continued to practice chi sao but also took up weight training. He always was a bundle of energy. He was like a small kid that would never tire. If he had his mind set to do something, nothing could have stopped him.

He combined weight training with his regular workout. He spent as much as four hours in his garage hardly taking a break as he worked on the equipment, built by his students to his specifications. Bruce was inventive and created several apparatus. He even fashioned his weight training exercise to avoid bulky muscles that might interfere with his performance.

For instance, he did not want muscles that restricted the movement of his elbows. "You must tuck your elbows in quickly when a blow is direct-

Bruce was obsessed with physical fitness, devoting hours every day to building up every part of his body.

ed to your midsection," he explained. "Some bodybuilders are so bulky that they have no way to defend the solar plexus area with efficiency. They can't cover the area with their elbows so when they use another method to protect it, they leave other parts of their body open. Weight training is supposed to help you, not screw you up."

Bruce concentrated heavily on his abdominal muscles because he believed that the body is "the biggest target and the least mobile. The more muscles you have around your abdomen, the more blows it can take." Bruce's body was covered with ripples of muscles. Broad-shouldered and narrow-waisted, he was an envy of even the bodybuilders.

To Bruce, exercise or training was almost a full-time job. While most people set aside a few minutes a day, Lee worked out almost 24 hours a day. Even while watching television, he would be in motion. He would do his sit-ups very slowly, his body descending slower than ascending. "You'll get more benefit by doing them slowly," he said. "It's not the number of repetitions but the way it's done."

When he wasn't doing sit-ups, he would be squeezing a rubber ball or pumping a pair of dumbbells.

Desiring accolades, many times he would ask a friend or acquaintance to place a hand on his abdomen or leg to "feel my stomach muscles," or "feel how hard my legs are."

Bruce used to say, "I want to be the healthiest and strongest 50-year-old man alive."

Bruce wasn't particular about what he ate. The first time I went out to eat with him, I noticed that he drank milk instead of coffee. He avoided cigarettes, wine and liquor but never refused a cup of hot tea. He would eat anything: pork, chicken, fish, beef, vegetables. His favorite dishes were Chinese and Japanese.

Although he was a small man, five-foot seven and 135 pounds, he had a voracious appetite. In a restaurant he always ordered an additional plate of food for himself—one serving was not enough. He also drank a lot of water probably because he perspired so much.

Bruce took a daily amount of vitamin pills, apparently influenced by the bodybuilding magazine he subscribed to. He prided himself in being so healthy. "You know, I haven't been (confined) in a hospital," he said, "so I don't know how it feels to be in one." At that time he was already 25 years old.

When Bruce died and the autopsy revealed that he had cannabis leaf in his stomach, I was dumbfounded. A few years earlier, he told me that he had tried marijuana on one occasion at an actor's home. "I don't want to smoke it again and I hope my kids won't touch that stuff," he said. "It was different and scary. I was feeling pretty high when the guy gave me a cup of hot tea. As I placed the cup to my lips, it felt like a river gushing into my mouth. It was weird. Everything was so exaggerated. Even the damn noise from my slurping was so loud it sounded like splashing waves.

Isometric leg flexing helped Bruce develop his formidable leg muscles.

"When I got into my car and started to go, the street seemed like it was moving real fast toward me. The white centerline just flew at me and so did the telephone poles. You just notice everything more sharply. You become aware of everything. To me, it was artificial awareness. But you know, this is what we're trying to reach in martial arts, the 'awareness,' but in a more natural way. Better get it through martial arts, it's more permanent. It doesn't make sense to be on pot all the time."

A few months after Bruce's death, Hayward Nishioka, former AAU judo champ, asked me if I had noticed anything different about Bruce just before he moved back to Hong Kong. When I replied negatively, he said that "Bruce called me up a couple of times and I felt he was on drugs because he was real high. He wasn't himself."

Bruce wasn't the type of person who would go against his own principles. When I heard that he was on drugs, I was confused because this wasn't the Bruce Lee I knew. Later, after his death, I began to wonder if the painkiller he was taking for his back injury affected his brain. After his death, the autopsy verified that he died from congestion of the brain caused by the painkiller. He was one out of a million people allergic to it.

Another factor that confused me was the sloppily written letters I was receiving at the end. Bruce used to have beautiful penmanship but the letters I started getting were becoming so bad that I had problems deciphering them. The first page would be fine but the last or closing page would be very hard to read.

I didn't think much about it at the time because he used to say "I'm so busy producing films that I hardly have time to sleep. This is the most wonderful time of my life. I don't mind the work. I can get by with three or four hours of sleep. My time is now fully occupied with writing scripts, directing, and producing."

Bruce adhered to certain principles, but appearance wasn't one of them. Bruce's attire could go from one extreme to the other—flamboyant to shoddy. Some days he would walk into my office unshaven, his hair uncombed and he'd be wearing a worn-out, old sweatsuit that should have been discarded a long time ago. But Bruce didn't give a darn for his appearance. If he and I would stop at a classy restaurant, he didn't care how he looked.

Other times, Bruce would be elegantly dressed in the most up-to-date suit and we might end up in a small neighborhood coffee shop for sandwiches.

Bruce loved to wear snug clothes. Actually, his pants were too tight on him. He couldn't put his wallet in his pocket so he used to carry it in his hand. There were times when he would misplace his keys and wallet and we had to search throughout the building until he found them.

His pants might have been too tight but they were stretchable. They had to be; otherwise, they would be constantly torn as he always had someone to demonstrate his high kicks for.

Bruce was not a big spender, actually he was very frugal. But when it came to clothing, he didn't hesitate within reason to spend his money for

Known for his iron-like forearms, Bruce constantly worked the muscles by pushing against a dead weight with his forearms.

the most fashionable attire. When double-breasted suits with the broad necktie attempted to make a comeback, he was one of the first to wear them. He was also the first Oriental man to wear shoes with high heels and style his hair long.

Bruce never had to pay for his modish hairdo, even when it was designed by one of the top fashion hair stylists in the country, the late Jay Sebring.

Bruce had a charming personality that enthralled most people right away. So when he explained to me that Kato's (of *The Green Hornet*) suit was in his closet at home, I wasn't too surprised. "I really didn't steal it," he smiled, "The guy in charge (of wardrobe at the studio) just told me that nobody is going to miss it because there's hardly any small actors who can wear it."

Bruce was taught early in life by his dad, a Chinese opera singer, that anyone with a precarious occupation such as an actor must know how to handle his money. "My father told me that an actor must be extremely careful with his money because some days he'll make a lot but there will always be a drought between those good days. He must have enough saved to carry him through the rough period."

Endless chin-ups were another method Bruce used to develop his great upper-body strength.

Bruce as Kato in The Green Hornet.

Early Years of Acting

11

"An actor's job can be boring, exciting, exhausting, funny and some-times even dangerous," Bruce Lee once said to me. "I remember that time when we were filming *Here Come the Brides* for television, during one scene I had to ride a horse which I had never done in my life. Actually, I'd never seen one real close up either. The only horses I'd ever seen were in movies and television.

"When the director asked me if I had ever ridden one, I replied nega-tively and showed some apprehension because he quickly smiled and said, 'Don't worry about it, the animal we've got is real tame.'

"After his comment, I felt less concerned until I saw what the horse looked like close up." It was ironic, here's a guy who fears no man but just the sight of the horse made him shudder.

"Holy shit!" Bruce blurted out, "I'm not gonna ride that damn thing; it's too big."

After several minutes of the director's pleading and the reassuring words from the rest of the crew that the animal was very gentle, Bruce finally agreed to go along.

"At first the horse was real gentle. As I was helped on it, it just stood motionless. One of the guys took time to explain how to control the horse but while the other guys kept yelling that I really don't need it as the horse was extremely friendly.

"As soon as the guy completed his instruction and stepped away, the damn horse took off. I grabbed the damn rope and kept pulling it but the horse kept going. I started to yell, 'Whoa!' but the damn horse never listened. It must have been traveling about 40 miles an hour.

"When it finally stopped, I was far down the field. I got off as fast as I could and was ready to throw stones at it. I walked back to the shooting site and the damn horse was already there waiting for me. When the guys saw me—how pissed off I was—they started to laugh. I was so mad, I couldn't laugh. I swore I would never ride a horse again, but that director got me to ride it for several more takes. He said that he couldn't find a stand-in for me. That bastard."

Bruce appraised the crew as pretty good. "I got along pretty well with them jokers," he said.

Sometimes, the stunt an actor had to perform seemed awfully silly. For instance, in the same episode, Bruce had to rescue Sally Field from drown-ing. Bruce was told to jump into the water and carry her out. "When the director yelled, 'Action!' I did too much action. I ran across the dock and leaped as hard as I could and landed too far away from her by at least ten feet. Before the second take the director warned me that I had to jump closer to her and, since the water was only three-feet deep, I'd better bend my knees.

"I was suppsed to be the hero," he laughed, "and had to save her from drowning. To make it look realistic, I had to lower my body till the water was just below my chin—as if I'm in deep water."

Bruce had a sinister role in the movie, *Marlowe*, which starred James Garner. He played a strongman hood, threatening and pursuing a private-

Kato

Bruce tutors actor James Franciscus on the set of the television series Longstreet.

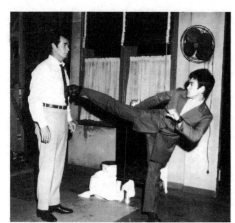

Bruce with James Garner in the film Marlowe.

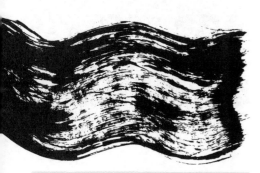

Bruce with Van Williams, a.k.a. the Green Hornet.

eye named Harper (Garner). The most spectacular part in the movie was when Bruce threatened Garner by wrecking his office, including a front kick at the ceiling lamp. "Smashing the lamp was no easy trick," grinned Bruce. "That was the hardest stunt in the whole movie. I had to jump real high and didn't have any help either—just a small running space to get my body up there. But it was spectacular, huh?" he displayed a wide grin. "Oh, the glass wasn't real. That's a typical Hollywood gimmick. Yep, it's made of sugar."

Like most movies, *Marlowe* had the same typical plot: the hero survives and the villain dies. Bruce's death came after a confrontation with Garner on the roof of a 50-story building. In a life-and-death struggle Bruce charged Garner with a flying kick and missed—the force carried him over the side of the building. "That scene was a real gimmick. I only jumped over a three-foot wall," he chuckled.

Sometimes an actor carries his rivalry not only in the studio but outside too. Bruce's emulator was Burt Ward, the Boy Wonder of *Batman and Robin.* It was almost prophetic that both men would someday clash because of the type of characters they played in these series. Their roles were similar; Robin was the ward of Batman and Kato was the servant of the Green Hornet. Besides, the public, mostly in its early teens, kept comparing them after watching week after week on the tube: "Is Robin stronger than Kato?" "Is Kato more valuable to the Green Hornet than Robin is to Batman?"

In *Batman and Robin*, Batman always had the edge of being more popular than Robin. He was considered the main hero in the show. But in the *Green Hornet*, Kato was the more popular hero. He was smaller in stature but did most of the fighting. When the Green Hornet was fighting one person, Kato took on two or three at once, using his clever feet to demolish them. "I had more fan mail than Van Williams," Bruce used to boast. "My mail ran as much as 600 letters per week during the peak period. I read almost all of the letters, but never had time to answer them. I let Linda (his wife) answer them. It was fun reading the letters—especially from the love-sick, young teenage fans."

As long as both shows were so popular among the viewers, it was unavoidable that one day Robin and Kato would face each other. The young public was clamoring for such a confrontation. "The director decided that we should participate in the *Batman* series instead of ours," Bruce explained. Bruce had no idea what the director had in mind, but after reading the script, his face lit up. He grinned and whispered to himself, "This is great, Kato finally gets to fight Robin!"

Bruce was a great kidder. He relished pulling jokes, especially on someone he didn't really care for. On that momentous day Bruce put on a solemn face. He walked around as if he was carrying a heavy burden on his shoulders. He hardly said anything and never kidded with the crew— which was very unusual. This was not the same Bruce Lee everyone knew.

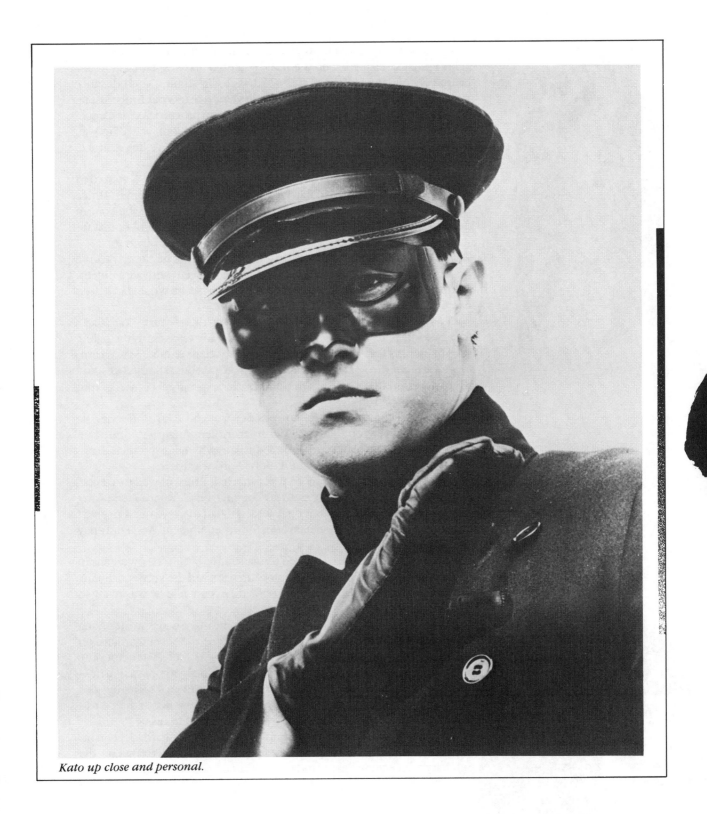

Kato up close and personal.

The Green Hornet and Kato in action.

When he got on the set, Bruce carried on this pretense. He stood in a fighting stance, clenching his teeth and squinted his eyes staring at Robin behind Kato's mask. Meanwhile, Ward as Robin stood a good distance from him and tried to calm him with irrevalent remarks but Bruce just ignored them. Finally, the director ordered them to proceed. As the camera began to roll, Bruce, retaining his ''deadpan'' expression, inched his way toward his opponent. Ward kept his distance and kept yelling, ''Bruce, remember this is not for real. It's just a show!''

Bruce had a helluva time keeping a straight face by now. ''I started to crowd Burt and he started to flap his elbows, jumping around me,'' Bruce described the incident. ''I was really scaring him until I heard someone in the back whisper, 'the black panther and the yellow chicken.' At that instant, I burst out laughing. I couldn't keep a straight face anymore.''

The director didn't want to dismay any of the fans so he cleverly let the heroes fight to a draw. Bruce accepted the whole event with amusement. ''Lucky for Robin that it was not for real; otherwise, he would have been one dead bird.''

Outside of the studio, Bruce and Ward kept up their rivalry. Ward had a little advantage over Bruce because he was already exposed to the public several months before the *Green Hornet* series came about. He was earning more money from the series as well as from personal appearances, and he was better known from the additional exposure because of the longer television run.

When Bruce started to earn more money from his television series, he moved to Barrington Plaza, a plush apartment highrise located in West Los Angeles. He never mentioned to me why he had settled there, but I had a feeling he did it because Burt Ward was there.

When the *Green Hornet* series was canceled, Bruce moved to Venice, California. ''As long as the bread was coming, I had no problem taking care of the rent,'' he said. ''But once it died, I had to move out. I'm glad I got this house, it's bigger and has room for my equipment. And I only pay half the rent, too.''

Bruce's interest in Ward started to wane after both series were taken off the air, but he still maintained some interest until the very end. Somehow, Bruce knew the whereabouts of Ward even while he was living in Hong Kong.

Even without the series, Bruce's fame became more widespread among the young martial artists. BLACK BELT magazine did several articles on his background and his skills in the martial arts. His fans were not only teenagers; now, they included the mature men. ''I always placed martial arts first and acting second,'' Bruce kept telling me. Even if his acting jobs were few and far between, he felt quite content because he felt that he had accomplished his first goal and was looking forward to his next.

In the meantime, it seemed that Burt Ward was trying hard to retain his image as a fighter and was losing the battle. Kato was getting all the publicity as a genuine fighter and Robin was completely dying out. I think

this is why Ward showed up one day at BLACK BELT's office to inform the world that he had been studying tae kwon do for six months and had earned his brown belt. When Bruce heard about it, he just chuckled and didn't make any comment.

Of all the actors Bruce knew, he felt Van Williams was one of the smartest. Van never made it really big in Hollywood but "that sonovagun knew what to do with his money," Bruce explained. "That Van, he's got it made. He doesn't have to do any acting to live. He has several real estate holdings and also owns a bank—at least, a big share of the bank. When he's not working at the studio, he goes to work at his bank as an officer. He has no worries about where his money is going to come from. He's one of the few actors with some brains and I have high regards for him."

During the periods between the *Green Hornet* series and his first big role in the Far East, Bruce did partake in some bit parts for television pilots and movies. "Some of the films that I was in never made it for syndication," he said, "but I still got paid pretty well for all of them. An actor has to place some value for his services. If he ever feels an offer is below what he should be paid—he should refuse it."

Bruce never took a job that paid below his previous one. "I don't believe in selling myself short. I'd rather starve than do that. I wouldn't take a job that is degrading to myself, my race or the martial arts."

Because of his integrity and high standards, Bruce lost several parts. When he was called in to do a *Blondie* show, he almost lost the part because he didn't want to break a board made of balsa wood. "I didn't want to fool the public with that kind of bullshit," he said. "I wanted a real board but finally gave in because they said their insurance wouldn't cover it and they didn't want to chance it. Anyway, after watching the proofs it looked real so I let it go at that."

Bruce had lost a great many jobs on Westerns. "Most of those shows want me to wear a queue and I won't to that. I don't give a damn how much they pay me. Wearing those queues is real degrading."

Bruce explained that Manchus forced the Chinese to wear their hair in a queue to degrade them. "When the Manchus ruled China (in the 17th to early 20th century), they forced the Chinese natives to wear those damn pigtails to mark them as women."

There were a lot of surprises on the set too. For instance, Bruce related to me once that the first time he was ever on a set was a real rude awakening to him. "For years I watched and admired this certain actress. I never thought I'd be on the same set or even get to meet her. Then one day, I found myself working alongside her. On film she looked terrific—good manners and real lady-like. But suddenly, she missed a line and blurted out real loud '———— you!' At first I couldn't beleive what I heard, but afterwards, I didn't pay much attention because everyone on the set used words like that. I think there were more foul words used on that set than anywhere else."

The heroes pose with George Trendle, originator of The Green Hornet.

Bruce studied as a youth with wing chun great Yip Man. Here he practices sticky hands with the master.

Reunion With His Teacher

12

One early morning in 1970 Bruce had a call from a major radio station in Hong Kong. In Chinese the announcer asked Bruce if he could spare a minute for a candid on-the-air interview that was being broadcast throughout the city. Bruce was ready to cuss him out for waking him up so early, but changed his mind and replied, "Why not?"

Bruce didn't realize the signifiance of the occasion until after he hung up. "Do you know we spent a full hour on the phone from Hong Kong to my house? Boy, that call must have cost them a mint. But it serves them right for waking me up so early," he kidded. "Can you imagine me talking to thousands of people way over there. I think it's the first time any radio station has done that."

"What did you talk about?" I asked.

He looked at me as if in a stupor and said, "Nothing important."

"Nothing important?"

"Well, I really don't know why he wanted to talk to me. First, he asked me if I'm gonna go back to Hong Kong and I said, 'Soon.' Then he asked me if I'm doing any movie right now, and if I ever plan to do one in Hong Kong.

"I told him that I would if the price is right. You know, we talked for an hour about nothing important," he said confusedly. "You know my Chinese is pretty lousy now, but hell, if it's good enough for a disc jockey, it's good enough for the listeners," he scoffed.

A few weeks later Bruce was on his way to see his mother so he could arrange a visa for her to live in the U.S. When he reached Hong Kong and was about to deplane, he noticed a throng of people. "Must be some big shot with us," he thought after seeing the media people among the crowd.

As he stepped out, all at once he heard his name in chorus, "Mr. Lee, Mr. Lee," they kept yelling as they quickly cornered him. Shoving mikes in his face, they began asking almost the same identical questions the disc jockey asked that morning during the transcontinental phone conversation. Bewildered, Bruce politely answered all the questions that were fired at him and posed smilingly with top actresses flanking him on both sides while photographers kept snapping away.

"Shit, I didn't know what was going on," he said. "But I ain't griping. I never had so much attention since the *Green Hornet* days. It's good for my ego. I couldn't beleive that one hour over the radio had made me some kind of celebrity in Hong Kong."

Later, the enigma began to unravel as Bruce learned that the *Green Hornet* had been playing in that city as the most popular show on television. "After I found out (about *Green Hornet*), it finally dawned on me as to why the interview over the radio and why the crowd was there. My mom had told the papers about my coming and they printed it.

"*Green Hornet* was a big hit with the people there," Bruce said happily, "and they kept replaying it for months. When I first saw it, I couldn't stop laughing especially watching Van (Williams) speaking Chinese. It was funny!"

The Chinese people idolized Bruce as a superstar. "I guess I'm the only guy who ventured away from there and became an actor. To most people, including the actors and actresses, Hollywood is like a magic kingdom. It's beyond everyone's reach and when I made it, they thought I'd accomplished an incredible feat. They think all who come from Hollywood are millionaires, too. See how backward they are?"

Bruce never got compensated for all his appearances but his trip was more than gratifying. "You know, I had a good time even if it was very hectic. My mom's place was bombarded constantly by the guys from TV and the newspapers. They came not just for me. My mom for the first time in her life got her share of publicity, too. She really dug it.

"I had the biggest kick when the largest TV station asked me to join them. The station could be classified as the CBS of Hong Kong. They wanted me to appear on one of their talk shows—like Johnny Carson. I went along because I felt that was a good place to introduce my jeet kune do."

The station was really pleased to land someone like Bruce for free and made an exceptional effort to decorate the set. "I recall that night quite well," Bruce said. "The station was so thrilled to get me, they made special props for that night and even asked me if I needed anything. All I asked for, and got, were two karate black belts."

Besides *Green Hornet*, which was produced several years previous, no one had ever seen Bruce perform—especially his current technique of JKD. "In a way, I'm glad they didn't see me," he smiled, "especially the karate guys, because they probably wouldn't have worked with me."

There were several guests that night but the center of attention was on Bruce. "Talk shows like that are easy to do. You don't have to memorize anything and can joke all night. There's no serious discussions—everything is light. After talking to me for about an hour, they asked me to show them my stuff."

Because the station wanted Bruce to return later, he decided to keep his demonstration simple. He had one karate guy hold onto an air bag and directed the other guy to stand behind him, explaining that if he should see his partner falling backward from the kick, be sure to grab him.

"The stage was small but I felt it was enough to generate some power in my kick," Bruce explained. "I had to stand less than five feet away, but everything came out OK. The two karate guys sure learned a hard lesson that night."

After instructing the two men where to stand, Bruce just stood back and waited for the signal from the cameraman. Meanwhile both men, who had participated in similar demonstrations before, treated their roles nonchalantly—not expecting anything unusual. The holder stood listlessly, leaning heavily on one leg while his friend, standing only a couple feet behind him, stood at ease with his hands folded and his back slightly touching the fragile props.

When Bruce propelled his body forward, both men reacted too late. "I kicked the mother perfectly, lifting that guy off his feet, driving him back hard. The second guy didn't expect the guy to fly at him and didn't brace himself. But even if he was ready, no way would he have stopped him. That guy was going too fast,'' he laughed. ''You should have seen the expressions of all the people. It was funny when the guys crashed into the props, knocked everything down. The stagehands were all shook up and ran all over the place trying to get the props back. But the two guys on the floor made me laugh the most. They were so shocked, they had the dumbest look on their faces. Man, the whole place was a comical mess.''

I interrupted Bruce and asked him if he wasn't afraid of a lawsuit.

''Naw, not in Hong Kong,'' he answered. ''The law there is not like in the United States. The people there never sue anyway. Besides, even if I get sued, it's going to be hard to collect since I don't live there anymore.''

After just that one evening's performance, Bruce became an even bigger sensation. Every time the phone rang, it was always someone from the newspapers, radio or TV networks hoping to get an interview. ''I think the whole damn city must have been watching the show,'' he grinned. ''I couldn't even walk down the street without people staring, calling or following me. The people in Hong Kong are different from the U.S. I don't mean the British, I mean the Chinese. They are more backward, like country bumpkins. They have no tact. When they stare at you, they stare at you and not just for a minute or so. They would stop and even turn around, just to keep their eyes on me—and for a long time, too.''

The morning papers had a complete account of Bruce's exhibition including his photo on the front page. The headline expounded that Bruce had found the secret power of ancient kung fu. According to the article, in ancient China the kung fu fighters were extraordinarily powerful and skillful. But this ability was lost when the art was carried forward from one generation to another.

''Boy, they sure can throw the bull!'' Bruce retorted. ''But you and I know better. JKD's got so little of kung fu in it that I can't, and don't, even call it a Chinese art. Besides, how can one compare JKD with kung fu? No comparison! It's not even close! Guys in kung fu can't hit or kick hard at all. Well, maybe that b.s. is good for the people there,'' he shrugged. ''Most of them just live day-to-day with nothing much to look forward to. Maybe, they can relate to something like that and be proud of it. Besides, it doesn't hurt anyone—it's harmless. But you and I know how I got my power. Yep, from here,'' he beamed, pointing at his head.

Within two weeks, Bruce had the whole country buzzing about his fighting skills. ''I've gone on (television) several more times but had trouble finding assistants who were martial artists. Those two karate guys won't come with me after the first time. I guess they didn't want to look like asses again.''

Even with all the publicity, certain traits remained the same with Bruce. For instance, when he felt gratitude toward someone, he would never let the person forget it. That was his relationship with his sifu, Yip Man. Even as busy as he was, he still took some time off to visit. ''Even though I realize that my style is so much different from wing chun (style of

Teacher and student in quiet moment.

kung fu Bruce originally had studied), to me he was the only sifu I ever had. I'm grateful because he was the one that got me started in the martial arts. And, besides acting, it's the only interest I really have.''

Generally, most martial arts teachers and devotees do not take too kindly to a colleague who has wandered off to another art or school. They take their art so solemnly that when a member expresses even the slightest interest in another art, they have nothing more to do with him. It's like an act of treason. They feel the ingrate is insulting his sensei, the founder and the art or school. But Yip Man was more liberal. "I have to give the old man credit," Bruce emphasized, "he was real understanding when I told him that I had completely changed my way of fighting because I saw the limitations in wing chun. He showed real interest in JKD especially when I told him that the style did evolve from wing chun.''

Bruce convinced the old sifu that the best way to illustrate his art was to spar with his students. When the old man consented, Bruce eagerly moved to the center of the room as the old man waved his hand, ordering his pupils to form a single line. Then he instructed the lead student to step out to face Bruce. "The guy was so baffled by my moves," Bruce said. "I kept moving in and out, letting go kicks and punches, never gave him a chance to recover his balance. I guess he got so frustrated because every blow I let go would have hit him if I didn't control it. JKD is too fast for wing chun.''

"The next guy got just as frustrated," Bruce continued, "because I kept throwing fakes and he kept biting. Once he got suckered and almost fell on his face. I didn't even touch him.''

While Bruce was slaughtering his students, the old man kept taking notes. "You know, the old man was really smart. He knew I had superior techniques and wanted to know everything about them. He even kept me after the session so he could ask more questions. He was really impressed . . . wanted to incorporate my movements and techniques to wing chun.''

Yip Man and his young protege.

Bruce was disappointed because the senior students didn't want any part of him. "Those mothers, they chickened out," Bruce complained. "I sure would like to have sparred them. These were the same guys who gave me a bad time when I first studied wing chun. I was a skinny kid of 15 and these guys even then were already assistant instructors to Yip Man. Well, I guess they saw enough and didn't want to make an ass of themselves.''

As the months went by, the old man was proud of Bruce's spiraling popularity, but his pupils became more hostile. "I guess those bastards think I should have stuck to wing chun and couldn't see me creating my own style. And I think they were getting more envious as I was becoming a bigger star. Screw them!" Bruce hollered.

Before the old man could utilize his notes, he died of old age. By that time, Bruce was the biggest star in the East. His movies were smashing all records. He was a phenomenon, not only to the working populace, but to all—rich and poor. He was a hero to the kids. To others, he was like a messiah—bringing pleasure and entertainment to their miserable lives.

Bruce was very angry because he didn't attend Yip Man's funeral. "You know those sonovabitches (referring to the old man's students), they live right in the city and never called me!" he fumed when I met him for the last time in May, 1973. "Dammit, they carried their jealousy too far. I found out about it (his death) three days later. I stopped by his grave, but it's not like attending the funeral. Shit, I felt real bad and disappointed."

Bruce always used to philosophize that all arts, like water flowing down the river, should never be stagnant. It has to metamorphose: "not change for the sake of changing but changing to improve." He practiced what he preached, too. For instance, just about a year before his death, he told me "I think I have reached my peak (in fighting). I don't think I could increase my speed nor my strength anymore."

A Bruce Lee collage: photos from The Big Boss, Longstreet, Game of Death, *and* Enter the Dragon.

Although Bruce seriously believed that he had reached his peak in fighting, he never slacked off in his training. Whenever I got together with him it was easy to detect that he hadn't slowed down a bit. Paradoxically, for a guy who thought he had reached his peak, his punches and kicks seemed to be more crisp. He might not have been aware, but even his concept of fighting continued to evolve—not dramatically but quite noticeably.

"Even if I think I've reached my peak," he said, "I gotta keep on going so I can be on the same level that I'm on now. If I slow down my skills will go nowhere but down."

Indirectly, he had proven his point to me during his last trip to the U.S. I visited him at one of the bungalows of the prestigious Beverly Hills Hotel. He was very jovial because he had just been informed, after four days of rigorous medical examinations, that he was in top physical condition. But to me, he seemed awfully run down. In all the years I knew him, I never saw him in such an emaciated condition before.

"You don't look so good," I told him. "You're too skinny. How much do you weigh right now?".

"I'm down to 120 pounds," he replied. "Yeah, I've lost a lot of weight from working day and night. I've been spending a lot of time learning the movie business since I've formed my own company. Not just in acting, but learning to write scripts, directing and producing. I've really been working my ass off. During the day, I'm at the studio and at night I'm writing scripts for my next movie as well as reading books on the whole damn business of movie production. Yeah, it's real fun and many times I'm so absorbed that I even forget to eat or sleep."

Bruce said that his waist measured only 26 inches. "Look at my muscles," he grinned proudly as he raised his shirt high enough to reveal his muscular abdomen. "They're still here."

Bruce was trying to convince me that his body weight was good for movies. "I think my weight right now is just about perfect," he said. "In films everyone looks about ten pounds heavier so that would make me about 130 pounds—a good size for my five-foot, seven-inch frame," he tried convincing me.

I shook my head negatively and said that he "looked better in his first movie *(The Big Boss)* than in his last *(Enter the Dragon)*."

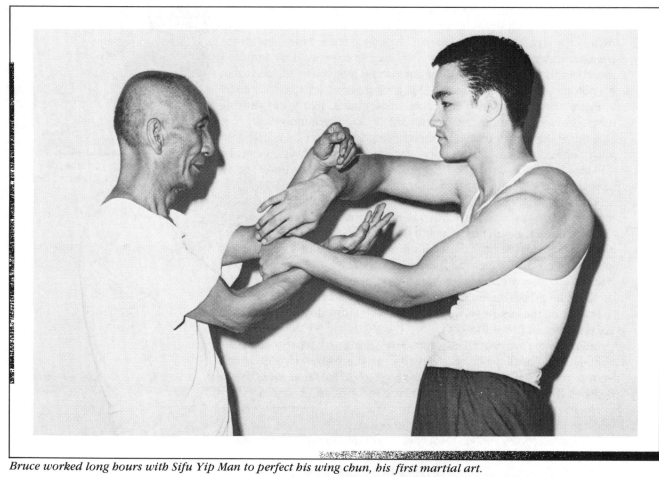

Bruce worked long hours with Sifu Yip Man to perfect his wing chun, his first martial art.

But he disagreed. "Hey, I might be skinny but do you want to feel my power?" he asked as he threw a cushion at me.

I gripped the cushion tightly and kept my elbow firm and erect as I anticipated a powerful blow. "I'll just throw a short right," he grinned, stepping close to me. Then he placed his fist about six inches from the target and without any warning, drove in his punch. The cushion ripped out of my tight grip and landed at the far corner of the room.

"Where in the heck do you get so much strength?" I questioned. "Gosh, you know you're stronger than you've ever been. How come losing all that weight didn't affect you?"

He laughed when he saw my confused expression and explained, "Size can make a difference but I've learned and just proven to you, that you can increase your power, if you continue to work out."

Bruce in a meeting with Stirling Silliphant.

The Making of Enter the Dragon

13

The first Hollywood event Bruce completely enjoyed participating in was the premiere of *Longstreet*, a television series which starred James Franciscus. "I really enjoyed working on that show," Bruce commented, "because it had so much martial arts realism in it. Maybe the philosophy and the fighting were exaggerated a bit, but it still had Asian flavor and I had a chance to work with Stirling (Silliphant) on the script."

Bruce on the set of Enter the Dragon.

Bruce only had the opportunity to see the "rushes" (early prints of the filming) because he had to leave for Thailand to do a movie called *The Big Boss* soon after the shootings. By the time the show made its debut in the U.S., Bruce had been gone for several weeks and his attitude had also changed. What seemed important at first wasn't so important anymore. Probably because he was placed so far away from home, and the location, selected by Hong Kong producer Raymond Chow, was a remote part of Thailand, miles away from Bangkok.

"Where I was, was a no-man's land. I couldn't think of anything but getting out of there as fast as possible. We were so far away in the sticks that they didn't even have a telephone nearby," Bruce said. "All we did was work, eat and go to sleep—early. There was nothing to do at night. No TV, no movie houses, no stores—nothing. I lost over 15 pounds that month because I only ate vegetables and rice. Hardly had any meat."

Bruce learned very quickly the differences in making a movie the Chinese way and making a movie the Hollywood way. "In Hollywood when we go to a location, we know who the stars are right away. They get all the attention before they even shoot. But the Chinese actors are treated very differently. "Until they start to shoot, you can't tell the stars from the extras. They have no chauffers, no special dressing rooms, no special treatment. Everyone sits together and eats the same food, sleeps in the same quarters and tries to do his job.

Bruce listens to Raymond Chow on the set of Enter the Dragon.

"The Chinese movies are put together normally in one month. The Americans take between four to five months or sometimes even longer. The Chinese don't believe in too many 'takes' like us. They don't go for quality, just quantity. Just slap a movie together from an idea—not even using a script."

Bruce quickly learned why it costs the Chinese so little to produce films in Hong Kong. Their top stars only earn about $400 a month, production time was extremely short and hardly any money was spent for traveling cost.

Raymond Chow and other Chinese producers were trying to copy the Japanese in their movie making he also learned "For instance, most Chinese movies, like the Japanese, used swords and other weapons heavily in their fighting scenes. But the Chinese were far behind in their camera work and also in directing fights."

Being in *Longstreet* was fulfilling but doing his first major role in a Chinese movie was challenging. "Their way of producing movies was so far behind that I knew if I could have a hand in it, that I'd really improve it. I didn't think the Chinese audience was ready for only the hand-to-hand type of fighting or the use of the martial arts weapons, so I decided to combine them."

Scenes from The Big Boss.

Another asset Bruce displayed from his experience in the *Green Hornet* was that he had so much ability, not only acting toward realism in the fighting scenes but also in directing. He had worked as a technical director in several films like *Wrecking Crew, Longstreet,* etc. "With a background of being an American actor and being the highest-paid Chinese star ever, my voice had some authority with the crew."

Bruce quickly took charge of the fighting scene in *The Big Boss* and rehearsed with each actor in the delivery of punches and kicks. He also taught each actor how to jerk his head at the right moment when a blow was coming. Too slow in motion would be a contact, too fast would look too fake. The audience would detect it right away if the swing to the face seemed like a mile away or if the actor moved his head too early or too late. "Sometimes, they'd have to shoot over 100 times just to get the right shot," Bruce said, "and we all expected getting hit in the process from time to time."

Bruce also had to teach the photographers how to choreograph the fight scenes. "Without the right angle, no matter how much you practiced, you could never put realism into it. The audience would easily see it."

While coaching the actors one day, Bruce was approached by an extra, Bruce learned later was a Thai boxing champ. The champ was so impressed with Bruce's skill, he wanted to learn jeet kune do right then and there. But Bruce refused because he hated teaching and besides he didn't have the time. "But it was pleasant just to talk to him about his techniques in comparison to mine."

It was sort of ironic that Bruce, who wanted to get away from that location and come home, caused the holdup in the production. One evening while drinking a glass of water, he squeezed the glass playfully and it just popped in his hand. "The damn glass must have been made cheaply or must have been extra thin," he complained. "I didn't squeeze it that hard." Bruce got a big cut and the production was delayed a whole week until he could use that hand again.

The Big Boss was his first major role in a movie, and he also had his first romance on film too. "I had to sleep in bed with an actress portraying a prostitute and did you see what they got for my first screen romance? Gad! Lucky for me I only had to pretend sleeping with her."

When the filming was finally concluded, Bruce received a pleasant surprise when he returned to civilization. He had learned that Paramount was desperately looking for him after the fall opener of *Longstreet*. "They couldn't get in touch with me for weeks as I was in the sticks."

Paramount wanted Bruce to be a regular on *Longstreet,* but by this time Bruce's interest in *Longstreet* had waned as he felt *The Big Boss* was going to be a very successful movie. Even though he got good reviews for *Longstreet,* he appeared in just three more segments. Bruce realized that his subsequent appearances were not as dynamic as the opening role. "When I returned from Thailand, the scripts were already written and I had no time to review or change them like I did in the first episode."

While still in the U.S. working on the three segments, *The Big Boss* opened in Hong Kong and became an immediate success. Now, Bruce was getting offers not only from Paramount but also from MGM and Warner Brothers. "All at once, I'm in demand," he smiled. "It makes me feel good, but I never signed up with any one of them because they all wanted to tie me up with a long contract. I'm in a good position right now. I can act in the U.S. or in the Far East—whichever gives me the best offer, I'll sign."

After the three episodes of *Longstreet*, Bruce left the series with no plans of being on it again. The series continued for a few more months without Bruce, and it finally disappeared from the tube. In the meantime, Bruce became a phenomenon in the Far East. His popularity kept on growing and he was the hero and pride of the city. Never in the history of Hong Kong had anyone caused such a rage. With *The Big Boss* outgrossing any movie ever played there, the producer's role began to change too. He was not the almighty anymore. Bruce demanded more lucrative monetary terms and more voice in his second movie, *Fists of Fury*. Bruce selected the title and took complete control of all the fighting scenes.

Bruce's original contract with Raymond Chow was amended. Instead of just receiving a flat $10,000 for the three films, Bruce was now getting a percentage from the second movie. Chow had no choice but submit to his star's wishes as bigger studios like Run Run Shaw were relentlessly after him.

"These guys there do business in an odd way," he said to me one day. "They don't come directly to you. One morning I picked up the paper and saw a front-page headline that Run Run Shaw was offering me $2,000 per movie, the highest amount ever offered an actor in Hong Kong. To play his game, I called up the paper right away and told them that I refused to work for such a small amount.

"Next morning, the headlines read that I refused the offer of $2,000. The following day another offer came from Shaw, a slightly higher figure, but I finally stopped the bullshit by telling the editor of the paper that I'd never work for Run Run, no matter what he offered."

Beside receiving more money and more voice in the directing, Bruce was able to dictate who he could add to the crew. In *Fists of Fury* he hired Bruce Baker of Stockton, California, to play the part of a Russian brute. To Bruce, the acting in Chinese movies was not as vital as getting authentic martial artists to perform their skills in the fighting scenes. To him, the Chinese audience demanded action films and why not give them the best of that. Baker was his student and also a friend who did a commendable job. In the subsequent movies, including the classic *Enter the Dragon*, Bruce used a lot of martial artists, such as Chuck Norris in *Way of the Dragon*, Bob Walls and Jim Kelly in *Enter the Dragon* and Dan Inosanto in *Game of Death*.

When *Fists of Fury* broke the record set by *The Big Boss*, Bruce was now in an enviable position. He was the hottest figure in Hong Kong's in-

Bruce is dwarfed by basketball star Lew Alcindor, who would later become Kareem Abdul-Jabbar.

Ouch! Bruce delivers a painful kick during a fight scene.

Bruce with actor John Saxon and Robert Clouse.

dustry. "I'm really enjoying the position I'm at now," he rejoiced. "I could go down to any bank right now and get a loan for as much as I want, up to six million dollars with just my signature."

Bruce always wanted to be the initiator in whatever he undertook. He was the first to take a full staff to Italy to film *Way of the Dragon* or *Return of the Dragon.* "You know that's the first time anyone from Hong Kong ever used Europe for a location," he boasted. "I also hired a Japanese photographer on the trip, a first for a Chinese movie. The Japanese were far ahead of the Chinese in filmmaking, especially in the use of the camera, so I hired one even though I knew we might have a communication problem. But we got by, we just used our hands instead of our mouths." During the production, Bruce was the first to use rushes in color. Up until then, all the major studios in Hong Kong used black and white.

The third movie was Bruce's first attempt at literally doing the whole film by himself. He wrote the script, directed the movie, and hired the main actors. It was also the first movie produced by his newly established firm, Concord. He and Chow were the sole owners. Originally the movie was called *Enter the Dragon*, but Bruce replaced it later with *Way* when the American producers who were doing a martial arts movie with Bruce had trouble finding a suitable title for theirs. Bruce let them use *Enter.* But by the time *Enter the Dragon* played in the U.S., it was changed again and renamed, *The Return of the Dragon* because *Enter* played there first.

While doing *Way of the Dragon,* Bruce and Chow's relationship began to fall apart. According to Jhoon Rhee, Bruce was very friendly with the crew "but gave Chow and his directors a bad time. I felt sorry for Chow because Bruce treated him like a servant sometimes."

The newspapers in Hong Kong even had an article that Bruce once threatened to kill Lo Wei, Chow's director. According to the paper, Lo had to run for his life as Bruce came after him with a knife. Rhee thinks the story was grossly exaggerated. "Why would Bruce need any kind of weapon against Lo? Bruce needed just one punch and would have hurt him. If Bruce really wanted to hurt Lo, no way could he run away from him. Bruce was too fast."

As soon as *Way of the Dragon* was completed, Bruce immediately worked on *Game of Death* because Kareem Abdul-Jabbar was visiting Hong Kong then. Without any script, he had all the action shots taken, expecting to write the script later. But all the time they were shooting he already had in his mind how the story would unfold. Bruce did not beleive in keeping his plot rigid. Even if he had a script but found that a change could enhance the film, he would not hesitate to deviate from the script. Sometimes, he had to discard hundreds of feet of film footage.

While doing *Way of the Dragon,* he noticed a cat on the top of the Colosseum wall stretching. A thought flashed in his mind and he immediately stopped all action. After getting enough of the cat, Bruce resumed his acting with Chuck Norris but changed some of the scenes. Bruce wanted to project on screen that he was like a cat fighting Norris.

Bruce had the film edited so that cat's actions were interrelated with his, but unfortunately, it didn't succeed in the finished product.

Way of the Dragon was the most expensive movie ever produced by a Chinese studio. It cost more than $150,000. "But I wasn't worried," Bruce replied confidently, "because we had already sold the rights to Taiwan for that amount before we even left for Europe."

Bruce never in his life had plunged into anything as intensely as the projects he was in. He became so obsessed with his work that he neglected his health. He continued to jog and work out, but he hardly took time to sleep or rest.

When Fred Weintraub stopped by to negotiate with Bruce to do *Enter the Dragon*, he was flabbergasted to see his friend so pale and emaciated. "You can't keep this up," he scolded Bruce. "You better slow down and pass the work around to others. Moviemaking is hard work and it takes several people to put one together. You can't keep writing the script, producing, directing and still be the main actor. You won't be any good to anyone if you continue to work your ass off."

When Bruce returned to the U.S. to discuss the contract with his attorney for the upcoming movie *Enter the Dragon,* he had a slight reprieve from work. But his stay in the U.S. was too short. The producers wanted to get on it right away as Bruce was such a hot property then.

Bruce was also determined to work on the film immediately because his dream was becoming a reality now. "I can just feel it in my soul that this movie is gonna put me right up there," he said elatedly. "With Warner Brothers behind this project, it can't miss! I'm gonna be an international star."

The budget for the movie was much bigger than those he was producing. Warner promised to finance the project with $500,000—a small sum in the U.S. but an almost incredible amount in Hong Kong. "I think that's the most anyone would spend to do a martial arts movie," Bruce said.

Bruce supplied most of the extras and also those with martial arts expertise. The producers selected the main Hollywood actors as well as the directors. The shooting was done in Hong Kong but most of the dubbing was made in the U.S.

"To get extras was easy," Bruce chuckled. "All we had to to was drive a big truck to the wino district and pick them up. They were real eager to work for $1.50 an hour. Believe me, some of those extras you saw in the film behind the bars were really heavy dope addicts. They weren't acting, that's what they really look like."

According to Jim Kelly, one of the main actors in the movie, those extras really earned their money because they took a great deal of punishment for measly pay. Nobody in the U.S. would take it.

Bruce agreed with Kelly. Many of the extras got slightly injured during production. "Some of the guys got hurt because they didn't follow instructions. For example," Bruce continued, "one guy was supposed to grab me from behind and when I used my elbow on him, he was instructed to let go. But that dummy just kept hanging on to me and I had no

The moviemaker at work.

Bruce with director Lo Wei.

Martial artist Jim Kelly.

Bruce takes on a crowd.

choice but to throw him over my shoulder. I think he got hurt in the fall but that's his fault. He got his instruction but I must admit that we didn't rehearse much.''

The schedule of *Enter the Dragon* fell behind several weeks and near the end, the crew had to work almost around the clock. "We fell quite a bit behind and each extra day was costing Warner Brothers additional bucks. When we finally finished, we did spend slightly over the budget.''

There were several mishaps in the production and they had contributed to the delay. Bruce gashed his foot during one shooting. "That dumb Bob (Wall). I told him that I was gonna kick the broken bottle out of his hand and we practiced it several times. But when they started shooting, I kicked his hand but instead of letting the bottle go, he hung on to it. Shit, I got an ugly gash on my foot and it took a whole month before it healed.

"Hong Kong's production was not like Hollywood. When we use a bottle, it's the real thing. No fake. If you remember one scene in *Enter the Dragon* where a huge glass window shattered in the radio room; that glass was not fake either. We can't afford to buy artificial glass.

"The snake we used in the show was not poisonous, nor was it trained. I guess I must have been unlucky because even the snake didn't like me. When I tried to sneak the snake into the radio room, the damn thing fell asleep on me. So I tried to wake it up by slapping its head and instead got bitten on my hand.''

There were some amusing incidents on the production, too. When Bruce tried to put one of his ideas into the movie, it almost backfired. During one scene a karate black belt challenges Bruce to a fight. Bruce tries to avoid him but the bully keeps pressing him. When the challenger asks him what his style is, Bruce replies, "that art of fighting without fighting.''

Bruce then tricks the bully into boarding a small boat so they can fight on an island. When he obliges, Bruce lets the boat out and that's when the fun began. "The guy was to remain in the boat until we reached our destination. But that day the sea was so choppy, water was filling the boat. We didn't know that until he started to wave his hands and cuss at us. The script didn't call for that.

"When we finally realized what he was trying to tell us, we had a good laugh because a few more minutes, that guy would have been in the water.''

Enter the Dragon was not a very good movie from an aesthetic standpoint; it was too farcical. Nevertheless, it became a classic to the martial artists. Most of the credit must be given to Bruce because he made it into a winner. People sat through the movie over and over again, not because of the plot or good acting, but just to see the performance of one man— Bruce Lee.

Bruce was superb in his fighting scenes but also contributed heavily in making the others look good. For instance, the villain Han, acted by Shih Kien, is over 60 years old and was not a martial artist. "I gave him a few lessons in punching and kicking," Bruce kidded, "and look what I've created, a fighting machine."

Frankly, Bruce wasn't given enough credit for his talent. He had so much to do with the success of all the movies he starred in from *The Big Boss* to *Enter the Dragon*. An apparent deficiency was easily noticed in *Game of Death*. When Bruce was absent from its direction, the actors performed, very awkwardly. When Bruce was present the last 15 minutes, they all performed much, much better.

Bruce Lee and Bob Wall battle in **Enter the Dragon.**

The proud author and his work.

Bruce Lee was a tireless worker, sometimes going days without sufficient sleep and decent meals while involved with a pet project.

The Path to Destiny

14

In early 1970 Bruce visited a female astrologer who was a favorite of Hollywood celebrities. She was supposed to predict the future with uncanny accuracy. Although Bruce was short of funds from being laid up with a back ailment, he drove all the way from his home in Los Angeles to Las Vegas to meet her.

Lee at work in his office.

Bruce felt the money paid to her was well spent. "Yeah, it costs me $40, but it was worth it," he said jubilantly. "The lady said that I'm gonna be very successful very soon—anytime now and I really believe her. I can just feel it here," he chuckled exultantly pounding his chest. "She said my success will be so great that it's almost incredible. My career will zoom so high and I'm gonna be a real big movie star."

I really believe that this lady astrologer influenced Bruce more than anyone else. Just after his meeting, his zeal to succeed almost became an obsession. He kept talking about his coming success daily. I'm not sure whether he was trying to psych himself up or not, but it seemed to work. His whole life began to be much more favorable. Soon after, he was hired for a good part in *Longstreet* with James Franciscus. Before the debut of this episode on television, Bruce had already departed for Thailand to do his first major role in *Big Boss*, a flick produced by a Hong Kong firm. Miraculously, the prediction began to unfold. For the first time in his career, Bruce received rave reviews for his acting. And for the first time, he didn't have to pursue others for work; the major movie companies began to seek his service.

The old cliche "when it rains, it pours" can be appropriately attributed to Bruce's later years. Everyone knows what happened after the *Big Boss, Fists of Fury, Return of the Dragon,* and the incredibly successful *Enter the Dragon.* Bruce's success was so swift, so overwhelming, that most young men in his position wouldn't have been able to cope. But I think Bruce took everything in stride fairly well. He became a little more suspicious of others, but generally he was the same person I'd known for years.

Since Bruce was a strong believer in astrology, I decided to analyze his horoscope. Bruce was born on November 27, 1940, and, according to Eastern astrology, he was born during the Year of the Dragon. That means, he should have the following traits: short temper, pretty stubborn, worrier, scrupulous, healthy, unusually energetic with longevity and a successful career.

Bruce's destiny and personality seemed to follow most of the particulars except for the longevity part which was cut very short. Bruce was a health fanatic. When I first met him, I still remember him as being the only person requesting milk while we all drank coffee at a restaurant. "No, I don't drink coffee or alcohol," he apologized graciously. "They're bad for my body." But he never found tea as a detriment to his health. He consumed it regularly.

Although Bruce was, to a certain extent, a health enthusiast, I don't think he could be classified as an extremist. He consumed vitamins regularly, many times more than the recommended amount. But he wasn't particular as far as eating a balanced diet. For a small man, he was a

A clever photographer turns the lens on the press during another of Lee's endless series of photo sessions.

voracious eater. He usually ate two servings at one sitting. Although he was game to try any kind of dish, he preferred Oriental food.

Bruce had a short temper and could be quite obstinate. He usually won all the arguments, but then, nobody wanted to get into a heated argument with him. His wife Linda learned early that "you don't argue with Bruce if you can avoid it."

For one who had a short temper, it was amazing how he could avoid getting into fights. He had scraps, plenty of them, while he was in his teens, but as he matured, he avoided them. "Shit, think of how many times I had to really control myself," he said to me. "After I made all those movies I got more challengers on the street than all the years in the U.S. There were young punks to old men trying to get into a fight almost daily. I know some of them were kung fu instructors, especially the old men.

They were all willing to fight me because they wanted to make a name for themselves. Whether they got their butts kicked-in or not, they had nothing to lose except risking some black-and-blue marks. Either they'd sue me or run to the newspapers like that Wong J. Man did in San Francisco and B.S. to them that they had beaten me. You know how hard it is to keep cool? Sometimes, I wish I could just let go and smash one of them but I can't with my status."

Bruce was extremely active as a youngster and adult. The only time he could keep still was while sleeping or studying. He could remain at one spot for hours if he had an interesting book in his hands. But normally he was effervescent, especially in company. He was very gregarious and the dominating figure in a crowd. He would pace the floor, throwing punches and kicks while talking and laughing at his own jokes.

He demanded a lot from others, but also from himself. For instance, when he decided to jog, it would be a four-mile, 24-minute run. If he decided to work out, it could be a half-day non-stop session. I guess Bruce would have succeeded in any profession he took up because of his tremendous enthusiasm. When he started to produce his own movies, he wanted to know everything about movies—from writing to photography. By the time he started on *Return of the Dragon* with Chuck Norris, he took over the production, direction, acting and even wrote the script. He stayed up almost every night trying to finish his task. Many times he just forgot to eat and sleep, losing 20 pounds during that period.

Fred Weintraub, producer of *Enter the Dragon,* told me that it was a full-time job just to direct a film. When he heard that Bruce was doing everything, he just shook his head in amazement. "Nobody but Bruce could do it. But even Bruce has to slow down one day or he'll burn himself out."

Although Bruce was mischievous, he was never unscrupulous. He always seemed to keep his word and I never caught him reneging. He was also loyal to his friends and to the martial arts. For instance, he once mentioned that he would not prostitute the arts for the sake of money and he kept his vow.

Some might disagree with that statement because Bruce did earn a lot of money from the movies. But if you pay close attention to his movies, you'll see that he did not sacrifice the arts for the sake of commercialism. To many, he actually enhanced the art to the gracefulness of ballet. Some of the plots were degrading and amateurish but the fighting scenes were done superbly, and in almost all his films Bruce was responsible only for the fighting scenes.

If Bruce were ever to prostitute the arts, he would have done so when he was riding high as Kato in the *Green Hornet* . He explained "several promoters had approached me to start a franchise using my name. They wanted to open martial arts schools throughout the country, but I just refused to go along because I thought the kids were gonna be ripped off."

Bruce seemed more like a happy-go-lucky type of person than a worrier. He never seemed to have any problems. But I remember once when he related to me about his fear long after the crisis was over. "When I hurt my back that summer and was laid up for a month, I really got scared because I just got Shannon (his daughter) and I spent a lot of money on the doctors for my treatment. I'm not afraid for myself because I can always exist, but when you have others to feed, it scared me a lot."

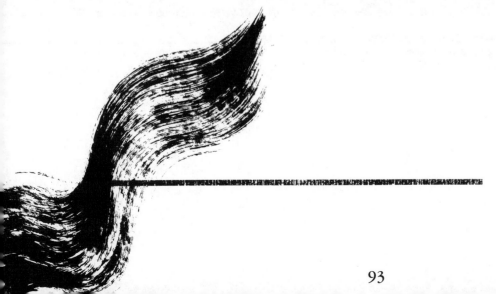

A somber scene at Bruce's Hong Kong funeral. Linda Lee is in white.

Astrological Forecast

15

"When Bruce died, it wasn't that much of a shock," related Mrs. Grace Lee, mother of Bruce, "because I expected one of my sons to die before me. You see, several years ago while living in Hong Kong I went to see a fortune-teller and he said, 'You have three sons but only two will be alive before your death.' Yes, we from Hong Kong believe in fortune-tellers."

Many Orientals from the old country believe in fortune-telling. This included Bruce. But he wasn't a devout adherent who followed it with a daily ritual as some people do. Occasionally Bruce used to see astrologers both in the U.S. and Hong Kong when he felt there was a need for it. Sometimes he saw them once a year, other times as many as three or four times a year. But he wasn't engrossed enough in astrology to read magazines or books about it.

Just after the 1963 visit (to Hong Kong) he said, "I knew I wasn't gonna see my old man alive because one fortune-teller predicted his death." A short time later Bruce's dad passed away before Bruce had a chance to see him again.

After browsing through several sources on the subject, I learned that Bruce's Western astrological signs were depicted more accurately than the Eastern. It's possible that Eastern signs have not been examined as painstakingly as Western because of limited materials written in English.

According to the Western astrology, for one born on November 27 as Bruce was, his profile would be as follows: Sun in Sagittarius, moon, Mercury, Venus and Mars in Scorpio; Juniper, Saturn and Uranus in Taurus; Neptune in Virgo and Pluto in Leo.

Bruce's strongest sign was the sun in Sagittarius which marked him as an adventurer who went beyond the ordinary. He supposedly explored and took risks physically and mentally.

During all the years that I knew Bruce, I don't think he ever treated his body haphazardly. Sure, he messed up his back one summer and that affected him permanently, but he didn't do it foolishly. He wanted to strengthen his back muscles and just used poor judgment while working out with weights.

Lee's grave in Seattle's Lake View Cemetery.

The only time I can recall when he took a chance of getting hurt was when he was in Switzerland and decided to ski. "I saw all these guys on skis going down the hill and I decided to try it because it looked quite easy," he said. "I didn't know how fast they were going down the hill but later, I found out that I was doing about 60 miles per hour. No, I didn't take a spill but I didn't see any fun in it either."

As far as taking risks with his mind, Bruce did try marijuana once during the late 60s. At that time he condemned the drug. "Pot does seem to expand my mind, but I don't care for it because it's done artificially and it could be dangerous. I'd rather expand my mind through the natural way —the martial arts. Besides, it (drugs) might mess up my brain," he laughed.

Bruce didn't gamble with his money. I don't think he even knew how. Frankly, he was pretty tight and spent wisely except for clothing. Like other Sagittarius, he was a carefree dresser and would spend hundreds of

Bruce Lee's mother, Grace.

dollars to keep up with the fashion. But on the other hand, he'd wear rags to attend a special function.

He was considered a non-conformist and sometimes his actions baffled his friends. For instance, just before he became a successful actor, he brought back a pair of furs from Hong Kong. One was a large black panther and the other, a tiger. I knew he didn't have that much money so I questioned his action.

"You think I don't know what I'm doing, huh?" he smiled. "I bought these skins in Hong Kong for a good price. The panther only cost me $5,000 and the tiger, $7,000."

I asked him why he spent so much money just to decorate his home and he quickly replied, "Look my friend, these animals are becoming extinct and in a short time, these furs are gonna be worth many times what I paid for them. They are very rare today in Hong Kong. I'm lucky to find these furs. The panther," he pointed, "is one of the largest in the world and should bring in a lot of money. I'll never part with it."

When he noticed that I wasn't convinced yet, he chuckled and said, "You still think I don't know what I'm doing, huh? Well, I was offered $10,000 for the tiger by Jim (Coburn) but I turned him down. That's a fast $3,000 profit but I'll make much more than that later on."

The astrological signs of a Sagittarius also included the love of traveling either physically or imaginatively. Bruce traveled a lot during his lifetime, but most of his itineraries were followed to earn a living. He visited Switzerland to teach jeet kune do to Roman Polanski. He went to Italy once just to use the Roman Colosseum as a backdrop for the movie *Way of the Dragon* with Chuck Norris. He traveled to India looking for a suitable location for a movie he was going to do for Warner Brothers.

But most of Bruce's trips were in the U.S. He toured the States to promote his movies, he accepted invitations to karate championships as their special guest and even attended a parade as the Grand Marshal in a midwest city. Frequently, Bruce flew to see Steve McQueen and Stirling Silliphant when they were on location to teach them jeet kune do.

Bruce didn't like to fly more than eight hours. "I'm not a light sleeper," he said, "but somehow no matter how tired I am, I can never sleep on a plane. I think it's the noise of the engines. That's why I hate to travel between Hong Kong and the U.S. By the end of the trip, I'm really exhausted."

"I'm considered a sleepyhead by most movie guys because I'm always sleeping on the set. Now matter how noisy it gets, once I close my eyes, nobody can wake me up without really nudging me."

Extremely ambitious was also Bruce's astrological trait. This one doesn't have to be discussed in length. Because of his drive, Bruce became one of the world's most respected and renowned martial artists. Not only was he an exceptional martial artist, he was also an extremely talented person who, as the stars indicated, had "gone beyond the conventional thinkers."

Before Bruce made his presence known in the *Big Boss* most Chinese flicks tried to pattern their action scenes after the Japanese. "The Chinese used swords because the Japanese did. They tried to imitate the Japanese movies but were no match. The Japanese were too far ahead in movie productions," Bruce admitted. "They had top cameramen, top directors and they used the best color films."

Bruce introduced more realism into Chinese flicks. "I tried to use my past experience in the *Green Hornet* and other films but was careful not to change the Chinese ways of movie-making too drastically. I got rid of the swords in *Big Boss* and instead used knives and other more practical weapons." He left some of the exaggerated human-flying scenes to appease the Chinese producers and directors.

"But using my hands and feet in the fighting scenes really revolutionized the Chinese flicks," he continued. "The fans immediately accepted this type of action. This is why *Big Boss* and the other movies I've made drew more people than any others. My intention was to gradually convert Chinese moviemaking methods toward the American. I don't think the Chinese audience was ready for a complete conversion right then but later, I think they can be taught to accept more sophisticated movies like those made in Hollywood."

Bruce was very optimistic even when he seemed to be in an abyss of hopelessness. Many in his position would have panicked and got a job or loan but not him. He always felt that things would work out and they always did.

His overly optimistic attitude emanated cheerfulness in his personality. I seldom saw him in a bad mood. His most apparent feature was a radiant warm smile to everyone. When he was present, laughter and loud noises were prevalent. He was a talker who dominated most gatherings. Unlike others with his exact sign, Bruce didn't get into many arguments and if he did he would display wit and humor to get out of the confrontation.

Many times I felt that Bruce's bluntness and hot temper would get him into more scrapes but somehow it didn't. But, Bruce was not the type to avoid fights if he was challenged. You couldn't bluff him because he would stand up to anyone. He used to criticize others, especially on the subject of the martial arts, without holding any punches. He was so confident in his ability to beat anyone, his cockiness showed as he said point blank, "Your technique is no good. You can't beat anyone by such a weak punch. . . ."

No one dared to refute his opinion because he was usually right and would prove it. But his attitude didn't help Bruce win friends among the martial arts circle.

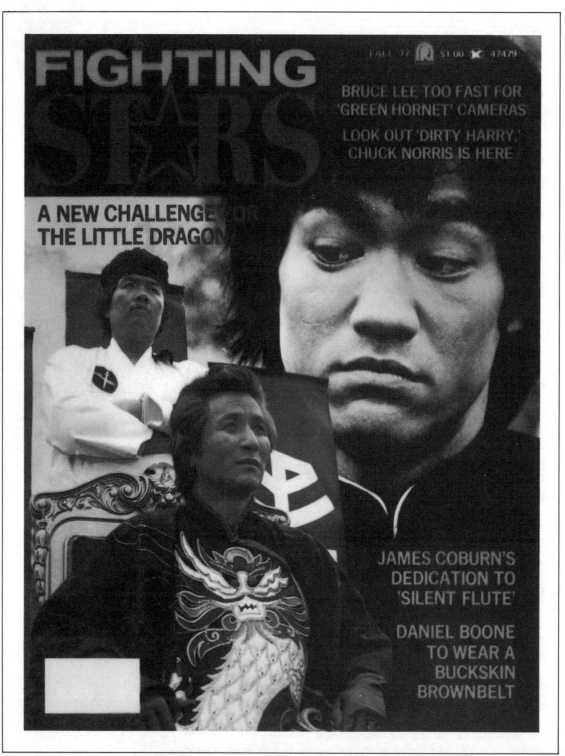

Bruce Lee on the cover of FIGHTING STARS magazine, looking over Bong Soo Han's shoulder.

The Rich and Famous

16

To Bruce Lee every day seemed like a weekend because he never had a steady job like most of us. From Monday to Sunday he routinely did the same thing: jogged in the morning, worked out in his garage, spent some time in his library—reading philosophy books, calling up his agent or his pals.

From time to time his routine way of life was shattered by unexpected calls from his celebrity students. One Thursday morning, for example, he had a call from Roman Polanski who phoned him from Switzerland to find out what he was doing.

When Bruce replied, "Nothing much." Polanski suggested he get a passport and fly over to give him some lessons. "He already had my reservation made and only gave me two days to get my passport and shots. By Saturday morning, I was on my way to Europe."

Bruce didn't mind this sudden traveling when it was arranged by people like Polanski. "It's fantastic when arrangements are made by him. I go to the airport and a chauffer is waiting for me with his limousine. He takes me to the finest hotel and the next day he comes back to take me to the airport for my connecting flight. I don't spend a penny and I live in luxury. Everything is so well planned that I hardly have to go through any hassle."

Bruce's trip to Switzerland was a memorable one for him. "I didn't realize how the ultra-rich spend their time," he related to me, "until I visited that resort spot in Switzerland. The rich have a boring life, too. Drinking and skiing is about all they do. In between, everyone is trying to take someone to bed. I was the only Asian there; all the others were Europeans.

Bruce also noticed several young girls in their teens flirting with some old men. "Some of the girls were about 14- or 15-years-old, making passes at the old guys who were at least in their mid-50s. At first, I thought it was kind of strange but later, I learned that morals do not exist there. No, those kids weren't their daughters. They could have been whores, I guess. I really don't know why those kids weren't in school. It was a strange situation."

Bruce mentioned that he tried skiing. There were slopes for beginners and for the advanced skiers. When it came to sports, Bruce always felt that he could do anything other people could do. Naturally, he chose the steeper slope.

Bruce amazed Polanski with his first skiing attempt. "I was going 60 miles-per-hour down the hill and made it all the way down without falling. I didn't feel any excitement in that sport so I never tried it again."

Most of the week was spent with Polanski—teaching and mingling with the crowd. One Italian industrialist, who was a black belt in karate, knew about Bruce through BLACK BELT magazine. "He wanted to work out with me," Bruce said, "but after seeing me throw a few punches and kicks, he asked me if I could teach him. I told him not on Roman's expenses."

Fred Weintraub

Before the week was up, the Italian invited Bruce to his home for a lesson in jeet kune do. Bruce demanded $5,000 a week with not more than ten students and minimum lessons of not less than two weeks. The Italian also consented to pay for Bruce's traveling expenses as well as room and board in a first-class hotel. But before Bruce could return to Europe again, he hurt his back and could not keep the date.

After the Swiss sojourn Bruce decided to stop at London. The royal treatment he received on his way to Europe was just as good coming home. When he reached England, a chauffeur was waiting for him at the airport. He took him to a cottage that Polanski either rented or owned.

The cottage seemed so inviting. He got the whole place for himself with nobody to bother him. Bruce was quite fatigued from the trip and decided to sleep late. But the following morning, "I thought I was alone and was surprised to hear shuffling noises in my room. When I opened my eyes, there was a woman in my bedroom.

"She smiled at me with a cheerful, 'Good morning. I'm the maid. I'm sorry I woke you up.' "

Bruce acknowledged her greeting with a smile. He was about to get up but he realized that he was completely nude. "I didn't know whether to stay in bed until she left or tell her to leave the room. I decided to stay in bed, but that was the wrong decision. She just hung around waiting for me to get out so she could do the bed."

Realizing that she wasn't going to budge, Bruce finally wrapped the sheet around himself and headed for the shower. The maid just looked at him and gave him the slightest giggle.

In London, Bruce roamed the streets stopping at every bookstore, combing the shelves for rare books. Eventually, he found a wrestling book that was written in Greek. "I was just lucky," he rejoiced. "They only printed a handful—about 16—in the world and I got one now."

"How much did you pay for it?" I asked fondling the well-preserved book.

"I got a good buy," he gleamed, "only $400."

I shook my head and told him that I couldn't see how a book could be of any value when you can't even read it."

Besides finding the book, Bruce also got in touch with someone very dear to him. While growing up in Hong Kong, his family always had a cook. But after his dad passed away and his mother moved to the U.S., the cook left the household.

For years his whereabouts was unknown. When Bruce bought his home in Bel Air, he wanted him back but every lead came to a dead end. Finally, he learned from a reliable relative in Hong Kong that the cook was supposed to be living in England. "I was so pleased to find him there," Bruce commented. "It was like a reunion with a long-lost friend. He was so pleased to see me and was willing to come to live with us."

A few months later, Bruce was able to clear with immigration and got him over. When Bruce moved to Hong Kong, the cook also returned to his homeland with him.

Bruce always mentioned to me that when it came to getting work in Hollywood, it wasn't necessarily your talent that got you the job; it was who you knew. So, with this concept in mind, Bruce made every attempt to know important people. One of them was Ted Ashley, chairman of Warner Brothers. Although he knew him personally, their relationship was more of a business nature. But from time to time they did meet in a convivial atmosphere.

I remember one morning Bruce stopped by my office and said, "Guess what?" he flashed a wide grin. "I was invited to one of those exclusive parties last night. There were only nine of us at Ted Ashley's place. Strictly for the important people in the movie industry. These men have enormous power to make a movie or kill it. They are the men with the money behind the movies. That kind of party is what every actor hopes to be invited to. Some would give their right arm to be invited."

Even though his relationship with Ashley was limited, Bruce was somewhat closer to Ashley's former wife, Linda, the famous photographer. Her interest was more paralleled to Bruce's, probably because she was more tuned-in to athletic endeavors than Ted. She jogged and played tennis regularly.

Bruce met a lot of great individuals in the movie industry but he reserved his highest esteem for Sy Weintraub. "You don't hear too much about Sy," Bruce used to tell me. "But he is one of the most respected men in the industry. Very successful and real humble. A real nice person."

Bruce's association with Weintraub was almost like a son to father relationship. Any advice Bruce sought, he depended heavily on Weintraub. "The most successful men in our industry are not actors," Bruce analyzed, "but the men who produce the films—the guys like Sy Weintraub and Ted Ashley. Actors are too unstable. They have such egos and can't think straight."

Although Weintraub didn't have a "blockbuster" movie at that time, he made his fortune producing most of the *Tarzan* films. Bruce said more than once that Weintraub had such a big holding in stocks that he could lose millions of dollars in one day and recover the loss the next day.

When Bruce was planning to produce his own movies in Hong Kong just before *Enter the Dragon* was being filmed, Weintraub offered Bruce $150,000 to be a partner, but the deal was never consummated because Bruce took in Raymond Chow. By that time, though, Bruce didn't need any funds either. He was already the number-one actor in Hong Kong. To borrow money was no problem according to Bruce, "The banks are willing to lend me as much as six million dollars with just my John Hancock."

Bruce visited many impressive homes, such as the McQueen's in Brentwood and Coburn's in Beverly Hills, but the most imposing home to Bruce was that of Byron Kattleman. "I never heard of this guy (Kattleman), until he contacted me to teach," Bruce explained once. "The first time I went to his place, I was greeted by his butler who had a heavy British accent. He was dressed exactly like the British butlers you see in movies. Kattleman was too old to take up jeet kune do; he was too out of shape."

Special editions report the fate of Billy Lo, Bruce Lee's character in Game of Death.

The host took Bruce throughout his huge mansion and when Bruce saw the swimming pool, he was taken aback. "I didn't expect anyone to have an Olympic-sized pool in his own backyard."

After showing Bruce the pool, Kattleman headed toward a small path that snaked into the wood. Both followed the path—which was heavily encroached by thicket—but soon came upon a wide open clearing. Right before their eyes stood a full-sized tennis court. "The biggest damn backyard I've ever seen," Bruce observed. "I never knew anyone could be that rich."

The association between Bruce and Kattleman didn't last long. "I used to go to his house each week and he kept saying that he wouldn't be able to make it but to bill him. I think I taught him only once or maybe twice and I was billing him $500 a month. After a couple of months, I told him that he was losing too much money and I wasn't coming back.

"The old man still wanted me to come back. He said that money was no problem—but I didn't feel right. Even if he's that rich, I just couldn't take the money for doing nothing."

Out of all the men in Hollywood, I think Stirling Silliphant helped Bruce the most. It was through Silliphant that Bruce got most of his jobs while living in the States. Silliphant opened and created many opportunities for Bruce in directing and in acting. However, it wasn't because of their friendship, it was because of the talent that he saw in Bruce. "I had such tremendous respect for his absolutely God-given talent, that whenever I could put him into anything I would just make up things to get him into the film."

Silliphant took his training with Bruce more seriously than the others. "When I first saw Silliphant," Bruce said, "I thought he was too old. But after watching his movements, I knew I could teach him. He was already in fencing (European style), and his stance with just a slight alteration was almost like jeet kune do." Silliphant was one of Bruce's first celebrity students and remained as a student for the longest time.

The constant taste of being treated as a VIP must have had a great impact on Bruce because as soon as he started to rise to stardom and began earning more, his standard of living changed greatly. He bought a mansion in Hong Kong and added several servants to the household. Even while living in Bel Air, Bruce already had the Chinese cook imported from England even if he wasn't quite ready to support him.

He even had placed an order for a customized Rolls Royce Corniche which he never had a chance to enjoy because he died before the car was built.

At the end, Bruce had so much money that he spent it to buy anything on the spur of the moment. But he also provided well for his family with shelter and insurance. Extravagant? No, I think he was more frugal than extravagant.

Superstars Lee and Lew Alcindor train together.

Superstars Lee and Jabbar

17

He ducked his head as he walked through the door. As he stood upright, his head almost reached the ceiling. Everyone in the office paused for a second to get a glimpse of the well-known figure who nonchalantly strolled into the display room of BLACK BELT magazine to browse over some books.

"Boy, he's tall!" I murmured to myself. "Are you Lew Alcindor?" I asked. He nodded his head sheepishly. I felt kind of foolish after I asked him that. "How could he be anyone else?" I thought to myself, quite embarrassed. But then what else could I have said to start up a conversation?

I'd seen him many times on television as he led the University of California at Los Angeles (UCLA) basketball team to the championships, but he didn't seem that awesome until I was face-to-face with him. (At that stage, he was known as Alcindor but later changed his name to the present Kareem Abdul-Jabbar.)

Alcindor had just returned to Los Angeles from New York to finish his last year at UCLA. He had studied aikido in New York under Yoshimitsu Yamada and wanted to continue studying the martial art.

"Do you have any books on tai chi?" he asked.

"Sorry, we don't," I answered. "But if you would like to know about any Chinese martial art, I know someone who can help you."

"Who's that?"

"Have you ever heard of Bruce Lee?" I asked. "He was Kato on TV's *Green Hornet* series."

"No, I've never watched those shows," he responded.

I told him that if he really wanted to meet Bruce, he should call me.

That night, I stopped at Bruce's house in Culver City which was about four miles away from my office. Culver City can be classified as a suburb and, although it is surrounded by the city boundary of Los Angeles, it is autonomous of the bigger city. But it is part of L.A. County and like its mother city, it is almost impossible to trace its boundary.

An old city, its population hasn't grown much in the past decades. Although the city is mostly comprised of older residential homes, there are also many newer apartments going up all the time.

Most of the residents work in the city of Los Angeles, but at one time, many worked at the Helms Bakery on Venice Boulevard until it went out of business. For many years it was the most dominating enterprise in that city next to the film studios of Metro Goldwyn Mayer. The daily aroma of fresh bread, which used to linger in the air, is now gone. The yellow, old-fashioned, square trucks with the rubber horns that beckoned the housewives and children are gone too, just as is MGM.

Bruce had never heard of Lew Alcindor either. "You mean to say that you haven't heard of him?" I asked. "Gosh! Everyone has heard of Lew Alcindor. He's the most sought-after college athlete in the country today," I explained quite surprised at his ignorance.

"How would I know him?" he replied. "Shit, I don't know anything about basketball, baseball or football. The only time I ever got close to an American athlete was when I had to walk across a football field while attending the University (of Washington)."

"Oh, yeah! I got to meet one of them. He was a big, awkward dumb guy," Bruce laughed as he tried to mimic the character. "Whenever I saw him on campus, I used to tease him and he'd come after me. He was so slow that I was able to make fun of him. I would dance around him and keep slapping his face. He would try to grab me but I was always one step ahead of him. He used to get so mad and frustrated, kept mumbling at me but I couldn't make out what he was saying. I don't even know how in the world he ever got into that school."

After a long pause, Bruce looked at me seriously and asked, "What's so special about this Alcindor guy?"

"He'll be the highest paid athlete coming out of college," I replied. "For someone that tall, he's supposed to be real smooth and quick."

"How tall is he?"

"He claims to be seven-foot-two but many think he's closer to seven-foot-four."

Suddenly Bruce pulled out a chair and jumped on it. He called his wife, Linda, to get him the measuring tape. "Hold the end of the tape to the floor," he demanded as he stretched the tape until he came to the spot seven-feet-two. He dropped the tape but left his extended hand in mid-air, eyeing the distance from the floor to his hand.

"Hell, he's not that tall," he remarked. "I'd like to meet him. I wonder how it feels to spar a guy that tall. Can you arrange for me to see him?" he aimed the question at me.

About a week later, Alcindor called me again and I informed him that Bruce wanted to meet him. This was the beginning of their friendship which lasted for several years.

Apparently, imagining a height of seven-foot-two and actually seeing someone that tall is very deceiving. Bruce was so awed by Alcindor's height that he kept muttering, "Boy, I never realized anyone could be that tall."

But Bruce was never impressed by Alcindor's sparring ability. "I told him to get into a fighting stance and attack me first, but he was too slow. He could never touch me. Before he could even move, I was gone—out of his reach.

"Then, I told him to be on the defensive," Bruce continued. "That guy had such long arms and legs, it was impossible for me to hit his face or body. The only target open was his knee and shin of his lead foot. He'd be too slow for me in an actual fight. I would first have to bust his leg and then there'd be no way he could have stopped me.

"But the only way I could get to his body would be with my kicks. If he should stand with his feet together (parallel)—his stomach and groin area would be exposed."

Bruce must have talked Alcindor out of tai chi chuan because after their initial meeting, Big Lew seemed to lose all interest in any other martial arts but jeet kune do. From that day forward, he became a constant companion and student of Bruce.

"Big Lew doesn't have strong arms," explained Bruce. "When I do *chi*

Lee doubles Alcindor with a punch during filming of Game of Death.

sao (sticky hands exercise) with him, he's very weak."

"He can't be that weak," I interjected. "Remember that time he got into a fight with a basketball player and broke his jaw."

"Well, a jaw is not that strong; anyone can break it if he hits it at a certain angle," Bruce contended. "But that sonovagun has powerful legs. When he kicks the (heavy) bar, it's just like a jackass kicking it."

Alcindor amazed Bruce more with his leaping ability. "For a guy that tall, he sure can leap. One day he jumped toward the rim of the basketball goal and hit it wth a front kick. I don't think there's anybody else in the world who could do that. If he started high-jumping, I bet he'd have the world record."

Alcindor had a keen interest in the history and philosophy of the Orient and Bruce's knowledge of Chinese philosophies made an impact on the young man. From time to time, Bruce would take him along to see a Chinese or Japanese sword-fighting movie. Eventually, Alcindor got hooked and would even sit by himself in a movie theater if he couldn't find a companion to go along.

Bruce also took him to see karate competitions, but Alcindor never seemed to enjoy them. One problem was that he couldn't stand the autograph hounds. Adversely, whenever he attended a meet, his name would be announced and the fans would swarm around him like bees to honey.

In the beginning of their relationship, Bruce couldn't understand Alcindor's behavior toward autograph seekers. "I can't figure him out," Bruce used to tell me. "It doesn't take but a second to sign his name. I don't know why he gets so peeved and upset over it. Sometimes, he can get real rude and just refuse them point-blank. For me, I don't mind it at all. Actually, I think it's a pleasure to sign autographs, especially if it's for the kids."

Bruce's appraisal of Alcindor's attitude quickly changed one day when the three of us were going out to lunch. Knowing that Alcindor resented being pestered by the public, I suggested a Japanese restaurant. I felt that there wouldn't be too many patrons in a Japanese restaurant that would recognize him. Alcindor was real pleased with my concern.

Bruce had an old blue Chevrolet at the time. The paint was turning dull from lack of polish. I don't think Bruce ever shined the car since he bought it. The only distinctive feature on the car was a sticker on the back window with the inscription: "This Car is Protected by the Green Hornet."

Bruce was very proud of the sticker because it was so rare. "Only a few hundred were printed," he smiled proudly. "I tried to get more but even I couldn't get any."

As I got into the car, I kept wondering how Alcindor could squeeze into the front seat, but he had no problem. He just slouched gently and raised both knees over the dash board. Later, Bruce told me that Alcindor's car is unique. "He took out the front seat and he drives from the back seat. I feel funny when I ride in it because the dashboard is so far away."

We arrived at the restaurant before the noon crowd; only a handful of

Lee and Alcindor pose for still photos on the Game of Death *set.*

customers was there. As we entered, all eyes turned to us. We sat down and Alcindor studied the menu, still feeling quite at ease because no one had bothered him yet. Unfortunately, his comfort was only for a minute. As soon as he had placed his order with the waitress, a daring customer approached our table for an autograph. Then another came, and within minutes, a line had formed. Poor Alcindor drudgingly kept signing his name on any material the customers could find in the restaurant—business cards, napkins, matchbook covers, etc.

When our food was served, I expected the customers would have enough sense to leave us alone and return to their own tables, but I was wrong. They just kept coming, not giving him a chance to take a bite.

Finally, Alcindor, politely, but firmly, blurted out: "Can I do it later? I'd like to have my lunch first!" The crowd dispersed immediately but that exposure sure showed us that being a celebrity is not all that great at times. I thought Alcindor kept his cool pretty well through all that ordeal. And I think Bruce felt sorry for him that time.

After we had eaten our lunch, the customers began to eye our table but Alcindor and Bruce quickly left the table before they could react. As I went to pay the check, one of the Japanese waitresses rushed out of the restaurant after both men, yelling: "Wait, wait, please. I need one more autograph for Stanlee."

Alcindor and Bruce kept walking swiftly toward the car, ignoring her completely. But she was persistent; she ran after them until she caught up with them at the parking lot which was about a half-block away. Although Alcindor gave his autograph, he was furious with her.

Lee dodges what seems like a mile-long kick from Alcindor.

When time permitted, Bruce had Alcindor on a daily schedule to jog and work out during the basketball season. "Big Lew is really getting into top shape right now," Bruce delightfully commented. "I got him to jogging four to five miles a day, lifting weights and doing our regular workouts when he's not practicing basketball."

"Does the training help Lew?" I asked.

"The shuffling (movement) that I taught him is helping him a lot and he says he's getting better balance."

After the basketball season, Alcindor still visited Bruce because he wanted to put on more weight. He felt that he needed about 30 more pounds to compete against the big basketball players like Wilt Chamberlain. Bruce placed him on a special diet and tried to coerce him into lifting weights regularly, but he didn't succeed. "Big Lew is too lazy," Bruce complained. "After the (basketball) season, he didn't want to train at all, especially with barbells."

Even though Alcindor didn't want to work out daily, he still came to visit. Sometimes he and Bruce would just talk aimlessly on any topic, but in between they still worked out. I recall once when Alcindor and Bruce came to my office. Both of them were completely drenched with perspiration. "What have you two been doing?" I asked.

"I got him to try out my trampoline," Bruce smiled.

"You what?" I cried out.

Lee in action.

"I got him jumping on the trampoline," he repeated.

It was hard for me to conceive a giant like Alcindor, all seven-foot-four, jumping up and down on that springy equipment without injuring himself. "You just signed a contract for over a million dollars, didn't you?" I asked Alcindor.

"Yeh," he nodded.

"What would happen if you had fallen off and got hurt?"

"Contract already signed so I'd still get paid," he smiled.

Just before his graduation, Alcindor began to seek more advice from Bruce. "Lew does get mixed up," explained Bruce. "I guess any young man, getting that kind of bread will attract all kinds of people. The Muslim organization has been contacting him and I told Lew, 'Religion is good for you, but there's more to life than just religion. Watch your dough, don't give it all away.' "

When Alcindor moved away from Los Angeles to join the Milwaukee Bucks, both men got together very rarely. Alcindor was on the move constantly and had no time for the martial arts. It was during this period that Bruce felt Alcindor made his greatest stride toward maturity. "You know that guy never had anything to do with the white guys while in school," Bruce said. "But one day he came to me and said that some of the white guys on his (Milwaukee) team are all right. I looked at him a little surprised and said, 'Hey, there's good and bad guys in all races.' "

Bruce also felt that basketball was good for Alcindor. "Big Lew always feels self-conscious when he's out in public, but around his team, everyone is so tall that he fits right in."

Sometimes the public can be cruel. Once, while Bruce, Alcindor and I were passing by a food vendor truck, the driver made a wisecrack at Alcindor. "Watch your head," he sneered. He was just trying to rile Alcindor because there wasn't anything over his head. Alcindor was real cool that time and just ignored the remark.

But many times Alcindor was faced with reactions from people who didn't mean to be rude. They would stare at him because of his height—not to embarrass him, but because they were just amazed. Once when Bruce and Alcindor attended a Japanese movie at the Kokusai Theater in southwest Los Angeles, "Big Lew startled the ticket collector," Bruce related. "The Japanese lady was real short, about five-foot. When Lew gave his ticket to her, she took it calmly and looked up at him. I guess she expected to see his face but when she raised her head and saw only Lew's waist, she snapped her head back instinctively and gave a frightened yell. I think she felt embarassed afterward."

The long friendship between Bruce and Alcindor began to deteriorate during the filming of the movie *Game of Death.* Alcindor was taking a vacation in the Orient and was determined to see Bruce. By this time both men were crowned with success in their own field. Bruce was the biggest movie idol in Hong Kong and Alcindor was the top player in the National Basketball Association (NBA).

When they met in Hong Kong , Bruce was busy completing *Way of the Dragon* which he produced almost single-handedly. He did just about everything—directed, produced, wrote the script and acted. Bruce had always been an opportunist and when Alcincor dropped by, he took advantage of the situation. Bruce influenced his friend to do a movie with him.

With only limited time and without any script, Bruce began to shoot mostly fighting scenes. For the next couple weeks, they spent hours on stage using rolls and rolls of film. During one segment, Bruce and Alcindor almost got into a scrap. "Big Lew got pissed-off because I scraped him while I was doing a high kick. I told Lew that he must expect to get hit when making a martial arts movie. There's no way I can prevent hitting him if I want to put realism in the movie.

"I guess Lew's trip to Hong Kong wasn't so pleasant," Bruce said. "At home Lew is a celebrity but in Hong Kong, he's nobody. People here don't know anything about basketball. When he first came down, my workers, who always made sure to take care of my needs, kinda ignored Lew. I think he felt slighted by their attitude although I tried to instruct them to take good care of Lew, too."

However, it wasn't until Alcindor insisted that Bruce pay for his transportation back to the States that their relationship really began to fall apart. "Shit, I won't give in to him. My agreement was that I'm gonna pay him for his time in the movie. I paid him for that, but I never promised to pay for anything else. He came to Hong Kong on his own, I never called him, so why should I pay his way back? But he couldn't see that."

Working with a tall person like Alcindor also took its toll on Bruce. "I had to take it easy for a full month before I could kick again," Bruce complained to me. "I was trying to get a perfect kick to Lew's jaw and I must have kicked at least 300 times that day. You know how high his chin is, huh? I had to really stretch my legs. Well, I finally pulled my groin muscle."

It was unfortunate that *Game of Death* was not completed by Bruce. When he died, he left rolls and rolls of film but no script. He had everything in his head and had all the intentions to write a story around the fighting scenes, but never got to it. After his death, the producer tried to complete it, but unfortunately, he couldn't do it as well as Bruce would have.

Bruce Lee didn't run everywhere at super speed. Sometimes, he drove.

Bruce Lee's close friend, actor James Coburn.

Coburn and Lee's Relationship

18

Everyone was in a festive mood. They came to celebrate Steve Mc-Queen's 12th wedding anniversary. No, it wasn't a huge crowd but it was impressive with just about every guest connected to the movie industry—directors, producers, actors, actresses, screenwriters, etc.

Generally, you would expect the conversation at such a party to be focused on the Hollywood scene, but not that time. Whenever Bruce Lee was present, he usually dominated the conversation. And naturally, martial arts would be the main topic. This party was no different.

One of the guests was James Coburn who finally got to meet Bruce. Coburn had more than a mild interest in the martial arts because he had starred in the movie *Our Man Flint* in which he was supposedly an expert in the martial arts.

"I had a few lessons while acting in the movies," declared Coburn to Bruce. "What do you think of that instructor the producer used?"

Bruce looked at him and grinned, "I know who you're referring to." Then, Bruce reluctantly but tactfully answered, "Let me put it this way, if I were to classify all the instructors in the country, I'd have to place him pretty far down the bottom."

Soon a guest, who knew of Bruce's prowess, interrupted and encouraged Bruce to demonstrate his one-inch punch on Coburn. Bruce eagerly complied. "Coburn is pretty tall so instead of my one-inch I decided to give him an additional inch. That guy was OK. Even though he didn't know what I was gonna do, he went along. I had him stand in front of a small sofa and placed a cushion to his chest.

"When I hit him, he fell perfectly onto the sofa, tipping it right over," Bruce laughed loudly. "You should have seen the shock on Coburn's face. He was so shook up, he looked funny. He made all of us laugh."

Disbelieving, Coburn stood up quickly. Then, his face lit up as he regained his composure. "Let's go! Let's go to work," he blurted out.

"Anytime," Bruce replied. "But I want to let you know that it's not cheap."

"I don't care. I want to start right away. How about tomorrow?"

"Sure," Bruce nodded. "I can start you off even if it's a Sunday."

Coburn became Bruce's most dedicated and enthusiastic celebrity student from that day on. "When I started to show him some of my techniques, he really wanted to learn everything at once. The first day, I got him to break a two-inch board and that sonovagun couldn't believe how easy it was. He was so pleased at his accomplishment."

Long before Coburn met Bruce, he was already deeply fascinated in the artifacts of Asia. "His mansion looks like a museum," Bruce explained to me one day (this was confirmed a few years later when the *Los Angeles Times' Home Magazine* did a feature on Coburn's home). "He collected antiques—vases, statues, all kinds of stuff from India, Japan, China. That guy really digs those things. Besides that, he's also interested in Oriental philosophy."

In the beginning, Coburn went to Bruce's house most of the time to work out because of the various training apparatus Bruce had. But later,

Coburn converted one of his rooms into a gym and began to furnish it with a heavy bag and other equipment.

In his training session, Bruce always seemed to combine the physical and mental aspects. He'd work you hard in the beginning of the workout and then after a while, he'd slow down and do more talking. There would be a sprinkle of seriousness but a lot more kidding around.

Coburn described Bruce as being: "A person who relates everything to the martial arts, or the martial arts to everything. He didn't separate life from the extension in his arm. And he's the only one that I know of that carried it to the point of really being an art."

Coburn believed that in the ancient days, there were a lot of practitioners who could truly be classified as an "artist." But in our modern era, he felt that only Bruce could be classified as such.

One day, after Bruce had known Coburn for several months, he brought him over to my office. Coburn—slim, tall, rugged, graying—put on a warm and affectionate smile. This was a characteristic nobody in the office expected because of the tough and callous roles he normally played.

Even Bruce had mentioned that Coburn got his big break when he acted in *The Magnificent Seven*, in which he portrayed a tough, cool character. "He was especially effective in the scene where he handled the knife real good. That scene alone made Coburn," he said. "Those who saw the movie if they remembered just one thing, it would be that part."

Coburn also impressed the office staff that day. He was extremely humble and took his time to shake each person's hand. He even went out of his way to greet the shy individuals. He returned to our office a few more times with Bruce and was always the same—gracious and humble.

Many noted actors, including Steve McQueen, would never frequent a public affair unless they were promised tight security. But Coburn didn't care. He used to go to martial arts tournaments and didn't demand any special favors. Actually, he was cordial to everyone, even to the autograph seekers.

Bruce and Coburn hit it off real well. As weeks went by, it seemed like Bruce was always accompanied by Coburn. It was almost obvious that when Bruce conceived the idea for *Silent Flute*, he would include Coburn. *Silent Flute*, which was created by Bruce when he was laid up after wrenching his back, had a profound martial arts plot. It was vastly different from the mass-produced movies of Hong Kong. "I think the public is ready for this kind of movie in the U.S. now," Bruce explained. "It's got almost everything in it. Action, intrigue, a taste of Oriental philosophy. It's one of those stories that you have to think out to grasp the meaning. That is, each person could interpret it differently, and all of them would be right. There's no right answer."

"There'll be a lot of fight scenes. Different styles of fighting. I may have to act in four different roles if I can't find good actors for each part. In addition to being good actors, they must be excellent fighters as well."

Obviously, Bruce had Sterling Silliphant write the screenplay because

Lee discusses a script with writer Stirling Silliphant.

he knew Silliphant was about the best in the country. Besides being a good friend, he had been his student for a long time. At first, he thought of Steve McQueen as the best prospect for the leading role, but changed his mind. He felt McQueen was too much of a star for the part and Coburn was more appropriate. Besides, Coburn already had some experience in martial arts movies. The three formed a partnership with both Silliphant and Coburn investing some money.

They approached Warner Brothers first because they all knew Ted Ashley, the head of the giant movie firm, pretty well. Warner Brothers was willing to produce the movie if it could be done in India. The company had a huge surplus of funds which it couldn't utilize. India, like many foreign countries, forbade its currency to be exported from its territory.

Bruce was delighted when Warner Brothers promised to fly the three men to examine the country for suitable locations. They spent a couple of weeks traveling throughout India. It was Bruce's first visit and it wasn't too pleasant. "I thought I saw poverty in Hong Kong when I was growing up, but proverty in Hong Kong is nothing compared to what I saw in India. I never realized how good we live until I went over there. Flies all over the place. Starvation, very common. People and kids begging for food, some lying along dusty roads, dying from lack of food. It stunk and filth was everywhere.

"You feel sorry for them, especially the kids, but you can't help them. If you give them food or money, you'll create a riot. It's really pitiful. I guess the tourists don't see half of what we saw because they only go to the nicer places. We went all over the area looking."

When the three men returned, Bruce and Silliphant believed that the movie could be produced there but "Coburn screwed it up. He didn't want to go back to India so he told Warner Brothers that India had no good locations. He killed the whole damn project," Bruce declared with anger in his voice. "I was counting so heavily on that movie. It was my one chance of a lifetime.

"Shit, if I knew he was gonna do that, I wouldn't have had him as a partner," Bruce shook his head despondently. "I should have gotten someone else. Well, we still may be able to have some other producers pick it up."

The next several months were very taxing for Bruce. His temperament fluctuated from hot to cold. One day he'd be on cloud nine, "Hey, we have a producer who's really interested," he would call me up excitedly. "We'll know in a few days." Then, a couple of days later, I would find him dejected. "That sonovabitch turned us down." Another day he would be elated again which soon turned to dejection. To experienced men like Silliphant, they expected it and took all of it in stride. They knew that it's a common tendency among producers to imply great interest and then quickly lose interest. But to newcomers like Bruce, it can drive a person batty.

Finally after umpteen meetings with producers, Bruce concluded that *Silent Flute* had to be shelved for the time being.

Silliphant makes a point as Lee listens.

Meanwhile Bruce was getting negative comments from others in the industry. They kept saying that he would never become a star because of his race. "The public can't relate to you here because you're different. You have to be white to draw the crowd. Maybe, you're better off in the Orient."

Bruce never believed them. "I'll be a star someday. Not only in Asia but around the world," he declared dogmatically. "But right now, I need some bread."

Fortunately, Bruce had a friend like Silliphant who always thought of Bruce's welfare when he wrote scripts. Whenever possible, Silliphant would have a part for Bruce. "Well, I contribute to his scripts, too," Bruce would add. "For instance, the idea for *Longstreet* indirectly came from me. I always had in mind that someday, I'd like to act in a movie in which I would be a blind fighter. I mentioned that to Silliphant several times and that's how he got the idea of using a blind detective as the leading character. My idea came from the Japanese movie *Zato-ichi (The Blind Swordsman)*.

Bruce never became upset if someone took his ideas because he felt that he could always think of better ideas later. He even assisted Silliphant with the first episode and even had a big role in it. According to Bruce, the first episode was supposed to be shown on the third week, but because it was the most promising, the producer used it as the debut. "Guess who picked out the title for that?" Bruce grinned. "Yeah, I did and you know where 'Intercepting Fist' came from, huh? It means 'jeet kune' in Chinese."

But by the time *Longstreet* made its premiere, Bruce had already left for Thailand to do his first movie, *The Big Boss,* and didn't learn about the reviews until several weeks later. The waiting was worth it because he was ecstatic when he received them. "That's the first time I ever been reviewed. Boy, am I glad they were all so favorable."

Prior to this, Bruce always felt that if Charles Bronson and Clint Eastwood—who were never big stars in the U.S. until they went to Italy to make films—could do it, then why couldn't he? But instead of Europe, "I'll go to Hong Kong and make it big there. Then I'll come back here and be a superstar like them. You just watch me," he said confidently.

Bruce's prophecy started to become a reality after the huge success of *The Big Boss*, and he never let those who discouraged him forget it. Whenever he returned to the U.S., which was three or four times a year, he would call these guys up and lay it on them. The actors, whose career had been languid, weren't exactly pleased to hear of his rapid popularity. To them, Bruce became a nemesis. "I can see some of these guys getting pretty envious of my success," Bruce used to tell me.

Even without Bruce telling them, most of them knew of his success because his name kept popping up, especially in movie circles, as his movies began to shatter record after record in the Far East. In a short period of time, Bruce singlehandedly created a market for martial arts films, not only in the Far East, but in Europe as well as in America.

Bruce Lee and James Coburn became fast friends, remaining in close contact even as both their careers took off.

Bruce was becoming a real hot property, when Coburn and Silliphant flew over to Hong Kong to see him. "They tried to persuade me to work with them on *Silent Flute* but I told them I'm too busy and not interested. Why should I? I've already got three hit movies, got my own production company and can get a million bucks from any bank in Hong Kong with just my signature."

Bruce never expressed it, but I could sense that he was still bitter with Coburn for killing the project with Warner Brothers. I don't think he ever forgave Coburn for that. "Why should I go along with him now? I don't need him anymore. It was my idea (the plot) anyway. If I want to do it, I can always come out with another *Silent Flute*. Besides, why should I take second billing? Forget it."

Even at the peak of his career, Bruce wasn't completely satisfied with his role. "Pretty soon I have to do other types of movies besides the martial arts. Steve (McQueen) tells me that if I don't, the producers and even the public will classify me as a martial arts actor. And once you are labeled as such, it's hard to get into other roles. I sure would like to do comedy some day," he sighed wistfully.

Bruce's utmost desire, however, was to be paid like a superstar. "When Warner Brothers wanted me after finishing *Enter the Dragon*, I spent over four hours on the phone with Ted (Ashley) hassling over payment," said Bruce, who was already offered roles in two more movies in Hungary for a million dollars each. "I asked for a million, but Ted said Warner Brothers can't afford it as I haven't proven myself here. He said that only a few actors get that much money now—John Wayne, Eastwood, Bronson and McQueen. He said they'd pay me $150,000 a year for life for each movie I do. He wanted five movies so that would be $750,000 a year for the rest of my life. If I die first, Linda (Bruce's wife) would be getting it. Not bad!" Bruce said and flashed a wide grin.

At this point in time, I don't think Bruce was concerned about being rich. He was almost certain that he was on the threshold of being extremely wealthy—wealthy beyond most people's dreams.

Each person seemed to view Bruce differently during his period of success. Coburn felt there were several Bruce Lees—not just one. In other words, Bruce was continually and rapidly moving upward into new phases or plateaus. At each phase, according to Coburn, he was changing, facing new problems, new situations. "It causes you to do a lot of things that you wished you hadn't done. So the thing that plugged him up, that bogged him down, was success. And that he had always wanted more than anything else; the success of achieving with martial arts without making any compromises down the line. Absolutely none. Finally at the end, certain things overwhelmed him—his personality got very tight," explained Coburn.

Bruce was brilliant in *Enter the Dragon*, but, according to Coburn, he wouldn't attempt to partake in other films because he couldn't act. "Bruce caricatured everything. His acting is too cut and dried. It is like the Chinese tradition of acting with heavy masks on and with very defined, rigid characters. He played the mask, rather than the emotional.

"It was a little overestimation on his behalf that he never learned to act. Had he learned to act, it probably wouldn't have made any difference at all at the box office. But it would have made more difference overall. I think it would have been a legacy of total artistry had he learned that.

"Bruce was the Ninjinsky of martial arts," Coburn continued. "He could do it. With the other guys, everything was done in quick cuts and a lot of movie tricks. To watch (Bruce) work was amazing. He was incredibly inventive when it came to fights. The only problem with the fights, from my point of view, was that he was always dominant. You never expected him to lose. So there was never any real conflict you felt that he couldn't handle. There was a lack of vulnerability. He was like a superman, which worked on a certain level. But to be superman he had to deal with higher principles. That's what *Silent Flute* was about; that's why we wrote it."

Bruce Lee and friends.

Superstar Steve McQueen, another of Bruce's close friends in the movie business.

Steve McQueen and Bruce Lee

19

"When I first saw him, I couldn't understand that guy," was Bruce's first description of Steve McQueen. "He was so suspicious of me and it took quite a while before I got to know him. But once he accepted me as a friend, we became real close."

At first Bruce thought McQueen's background of extreme hardship—spending time in a detention camp and coming from a broken family—had a lot to do with his behavior. But later, Bruce realized that this was not entirely the case. Becoming a superstar might have contributed more to his suspicious attitude. Even Bruce, himself, after reaching stardom, confessed that "many people attempt to take advantage of me and use me for their personal gain. I have to be more careful and be on guard constantly."

Bruce and McQueen's association was more on a friendship than a teacher-student basis. Although McQueen was one of his old-time students, he was far from being an expert. "I'm not an expert or anything like that. I'm not involved in the martial arts to any degree," declared McQueen. "Bruce was just a very old personal friend of mine, and I cared for him a lot. I thought he was a brilliant, fine philosopher about everyday living. He had good standards, and I have great respect for that."

Bruce also had high regard for his friend. "As a student, Steve can be good," Bruce used to tell me, "because he's a hard worker. One day I went to his place to work out and that guy doesn't know the meaning of quitting. He just kept pushing himself for hours—punching and kicking without a break—until he was completely exhausted. His gym clothes were completely soaked by the time we gave up."

Pretentious? That wasn't McQueen's style. "You know that nut," Bruce chuckled, "instead of taking a shower and putting on fresh clothes, he tells me, 'let's go to my office.'

"By the time we reached his office, our clothes were still damp and we stunk like hell. But Steve didn't give a shit. He stopped his car right in front of his office and I hestitated to step out when I saw his swanky office and all his employees dressed up. 'C'mon,' Steve waved, 'let's go meet some of the guys.' It was kind of funny, Steve looked like a bum off the street and everyone looking up at him and kept calling him, 'Mr. McQueen,' " Bruce laughed.

Eventually, Bruce learned that McQueen was not only a successful actor but also a prosperous entrepreneur. Besides a plastic company in Santa Monica, he also owned a motorcycle company in Italy and a movie production company. "Steve would be dammed good if he could work out more but that sonovagun never stays home. If he's shooting, he'll be stuck at a location for as long as five months, returning home for a couple days in between. If he's not working, he'll be somewhere in the desert, driving his dune buggy or motorcycle."

Once in a while McQueen would call Bruce to fly in. "The public thinks acting is a lot of fun or exciting. It's not! Actually, it's boring, especially if you're stuck in the desert or in a dinky town where the people go to sleep right after dinner. But a star like Steve had to work extremely hard. That's why so many actors turn to the bottle and become alcoholics. They start

McQueen, according to Lee, was one of the gutsiest, craziest men he ever knew.

at six in the morning and quit late at night. The main actors are always working while the rest—who put in a long day—just sit and wait. To me, the waiting is the hardest part. Get to work before the sun is up, and then have to wait until you're called. Sometimes, you're never called all day.

"Steve flies me in because he wants to talk to somebody else besides the same guys he works with all day long. I guess he gets sick of seeing them day in and day out. We usually talk about life, philosophy and work out a little. It gives Steve a break from what he's doing. No, I don't stay long, just a couple of days."

Bruce mentioned that many people think that the important stars sleep with the beautiful actresses. The practice may be going on but it's not common. "Guys like Steve, can't afford to ruin their reputations. Their stakes are too high. They put too many years of hard work to be where they are. It's not worth it."

According to Bruce, McQueen seemed to enjoy taking risks. "You know that guy, he must drive his insurance man crazy. Once, he got all banged up when the dune buggy he was driving turned over, almost killing him. Most guys would hesitate to drive that damned thing again, but not Steve. He couldn't wait for his injury to heal so he could get behind the wheel. You know, sometimes I wonder if he's not crazy." Bruce kidded. "He'd do things that even the most gutsy stunt men wouldn't dare do."

In the movie *The Great Escape*, McQueen did most of the dangerous motorcycle stunts himself. In *Bullitt*, which his company produced, he did practically all the hazardous driving on the hilly streets of San Francisco.

Bruce, at first, couldn't understand McQueen's motive of taking unnecessary risks. Finally, he came to the conclusion that even with all his success, fame and money, McQueen was bored with life. "I think he takes all those risks for excitement. That's his way of having fun. If you think I'm a fast driver, you should ride with Steve. One afternoon while coming down Mulholland in his Ferrari, he must have thought we were on the race track because he was going at least 60 around the curves. You know I usually don't get scared that easy, but Steve sure made me shit that time. I kept praying that he doesn't hit a stone or there'll be no tomorrow."

Possibly, McQueen and Bruce got along so well because both of them enjoyed studying the theories and philosophies of life. "He and I used to have great long discussions about that," said McQueen, "because no matter how expensive a car you buy, how many expensive clothes (you have), no matter what you do in life—if you don't know yourself, you're never going to . . . appreciate anything in life. Bruce was very much into that. I think he was very much a part of today's psychotherapy. I imagine he used the martial arts as an extension of himself. But he also knew himself in everyday life."

Of all the actor friends Bruce had, McQueen was the closest to him. When Bruce wanted to buy a house, McQueen immediately contacted his manager to find him one. After several weeks of hunting, he finally found one in Bel Air.

Bel Air is perched high in the hills, just above the University of California at Los Angeles (UCLA). The exclusive, quiet, tiny hamlet is almost completely hidden from view of commuters who drive along busy Sunset Boulevard and the San Diego Freeway. The easiest access (the only one) is Mulholland Drive after getting off the San Diego Freeway. Once inside the concrete gates, the paved roads narrow and are steep and crooked.

The community sits between Beverly Hills and Brentwood. It's not as big nor as renowned as Beverly Hills but it can claim just as high a percentage of notables as its residents—mostly movie moguls and high-salaried actors. Surprisingly, many, even those who have lived in Los Angeles all their lives, don't know how to get there.

Generally Bruce would fill me in on his important plans but that time he didn't. He just called me up one day and said that he was about to buy a house. "I didn't even know you were shopping for one," I responded.

"Hey, you're the guy who told me to get one. Don't you remember?" he chuckled delightfully. "Yeah, you told me I can save on taxes and make money at the same time."

Frankly, I don't think Bruce went house hunting on his own. No, he'd be too frustrated from such an ordeal. He was too impatient. I think he left it up to McQueen's manager. Nevertheless, when Bruce first saw the house, he fell in love with it. I could see why, too. The white cottage with a shake roof, surrounded by a low picket fence, seemed so inviting and comfortable. Even though it was outflanked by the more luxurious and massive homes, it blended with the environment—probably from the landscaping. His home, like his neighbors, was almost engulfed by well-manicured vines and shrubs. Several towering trees spread their leafy branches over it, protecting it from the hot California sun.

Bruce's single-story, three-bedroom home actually sat on a high bank of a valley. The front picket fence hugged along the edge of the sidewalk and a few steps back stood the entrance of his living room. The spacious living room was surrounded by elegant Victorian windows and a fireplace, constructed with decorous red bricks. The structure must have been several years old as evidenced by the solid floor and quality workmanship. The garage, which adjoined to the side of the house, was converted to a gym. It was so filled with his training equipment that it had no room for his cars.

Bruce's backyard was wide and deep. As he guided me through his property, he finally stopped at the edge of his backyard and pointed to the bottom of the valley. Exuberantly he cried, "My property goes all the way down to the bottom. It's over 200 feet down the slope. For all that property, don't you think I got a good buy at $50,000?" he asked. I nodded my head and smiled. I realized that he had paid a fair price for his home but I felt that the sloping land was hardly worth anything.

About a month later, I visited Bruce and he was just as jubilant as the day he moved into his new home. He was like a child who had received his first toy. "This place is terrific," he began, "I'm away from the heavy city traffic and still can get to any place in Los Angeles quickly. Man, this place is quiet. Sometimes, I just sit in my backyard and gaze at the ocean,

watching the sun slowly setting. Civilization seems so far away. I can just hear the birds and feel the gentle breeze upon my naked body. But the best view of the sunset is from Mulholland. When I'm driving down, I can see the sun setting without anything in its way. Even the damned smog can't hide the spectacular view."

Bruce related to me that he had trouble sleeping the first couple nights. He felt uneasy as he wasn't accustomed to the silence and almost total darkness of the place. "It was so quiet that I'll bet I could have heard a pin drop to the floor. Some nights I hear strange noises in my backyard or on my roof. Next morning I see animal tracks around my house. I didn't know that they came from the wild animals until my neighbor told me. He said the noises on my roof came from either raccoons or squirrels. It's kinda funny, all these years I lived in L.A. and never dreamt that wild animals roamed so close to us."

After Bruce had settled into his new residence, I thought he would neglect to run because the roads were so steep. "Me, not running? You must be kidding," he said. "I'm working out on the road more than ever. It's much tougher to run up and down the hill but I like it because I get more out of it. Running upward is hard but it's good to strengthen your legs and develop your stamina. But it's easier than running down hill. Going down is hard on your legs as you have to keep braking. You don't get too much benefit either."

The only time Bruce might have had to postpone his running was when it rained heavily. The main road, which crosses at the bottom of the valley without a bridge, could turn into a savage rapids. Sometimes, even cars couldn't pass.

The first summer in Bel Air was not all pleasant. His friends, Sharon Tate and Jay Sebring, were murdered by the Charles Manson gang. "The house was only a couple blocks away," Bruce pointed out. "Boy, when things like that happen in your own backyard, it scares the hell out of you, especially when you have a family. From what I picked up at the funeral, what they did to the victims was awful. Even the papers couldn't describe it. It was just too brutal."

I've read several accounts in the newspapers that Jay Sebring either had a black belt or was an expert in karate. I never met Sebring but Bruce had told me that he had taught him in the past. I didn't know to what extent so I got curious. "Sebring could never get out of a situation like that," Bruce commented. "He was still too green and he wasn't that type of guy who would fight back. He was a small man and far from being a fighter."

As years went by Bruce and McQueen began to visit each other more frequently. Bruce would call him at the spur of the moment, but to McQueen the calls were more than ordinary. They seemed to come at the most appropriate times. "Sometimes, I'd feel rotten and the phone would ring," McQueen once said, "and it was Bruce Lee. I don't know why he would call but he'd say, 'I just thought I should call you.' Now this happened four or five times . . . how do you explain it?"

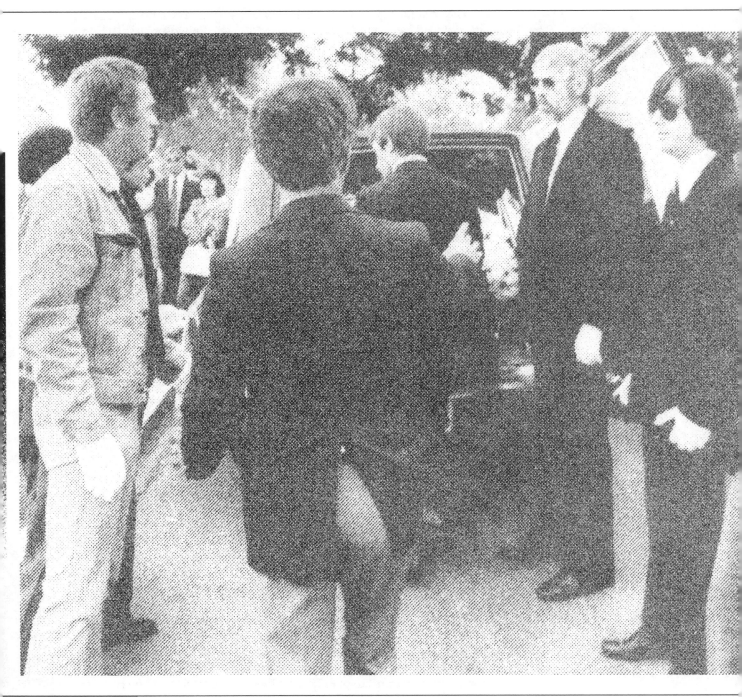

Steve McQueen and James Coburn as pallbearers in Lee's funeral.

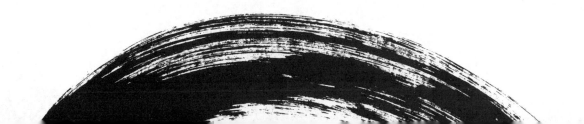

The relationship between both men was not always serious. I think they kidded each other more than they discussed philosophies. During Bruce's last visit to the U.S., I still remember clearly how he took McQueen's gags. Bruce was already a superstar and McQueen sent him an 8x10 photo of himself. "You know that sonovabitch, he sent me a photo of himself with an autograph, ''To Bruce Lee, one of my favorite fans.'' I tried to get hold of him and nobody knows where he's at. That chicken, he knows what I'm gonna tell him so he's hiding,'' Bruce scolded with a twinkle in his eyes.

Sometimes Bruce would stop by McQueen's place in Brentwood. "You should see Steve's house,'' Bruce chuckled. "He had to build it like a fort to keep the public away. Just to get to his front door is a hassle. His house is completely surrounded by a high steel fence to keep the fans or intruders out. When you get there you have to stop first at the steel gate where there's a phone connected to his house. You have to introduce yourself and then the gate opens automatically. And then you still have to drive several more yards to get to his front door.

"I can understand why Steve has to live like that. He's so well-known. His life would be a mess if people are able to come up to his front door. He'd never have rest.''

Even though McQueen shunned the public, he didn't attempt to disguise himself deliberately when he visited Bruce. McQueen's taste for vehicles varied and Bruce never knew how he'd come. One day, McQueen came on a motorcycle to Bruce's Culver City home. "Damn Steve, he finally got caught,'' Bruce laughed out loud. "He came to my house on his souped-up bike that woke up the whole neighborhood. No one could recognize him, even me, until he took his goggles and helmet off. He rode this big sucker with the handlebars real low, the seat way up so he had to drive with his ass way up. Anyway, a few minutes after he left me, I got a phone call. It was Steve on the other end griping like hell that he got a ticket just a few blocks from my house. He said that when he left, the cops had a roadblock waiting for him. Seems they had seen him driving like a maniac coming to my house but lost him so they just waited. His ticket read that he was driving 80 in a 25 mph zone.

"Besides the souped-up motorcycle, he also has a beat-up old car which carries an engine that belongs in a racing car,'' Bruce continued. "But he's also got an expensive Ferrari and other cars including a dune buggy.''

I don't think Bruce charged McQueen for lessons, although he got as much as $100 an hour from the other celebrities. Bruce gave me the impression that he and Steve had an implied agreement. "I teach Steve jeet kune do and he gives me advice on acting. No, he doesn't try to convert me to his style. He believes that each actor must create his own style. You can't learn that from anyone. That's why he doesn't feel that you can get too much out of the playhouses. The other actors got pretty mad at him because he wouldn't support them. He tells me that it's more important that I meet the right people in the industry.''

At the peak of his career, Bruce had turned off some of his actor-friends. "Yeah, some of the guys don't want me to talk about my big success in the movies. I can feel the envy in them," Bruce related. "But that Steve is OK. He was real happy for me and tried to help because he knows the problems that I'm gonna face."

The friendship between the two was established long before this. When Bruce wanted to buy a Porsche, McQueen quickly volunteered to pay for the car. Later, when Bruce was planning to buy the house that McQueen's manager found, he offered to pay for the down payment. "That Steve is too much," Bruce said, shaking his head. "He wanted to pay for the down payment but I couldn't accept. You know how much that was? Ten grand! Boy, that's a lot of money and he was just gonna give it to me with no strings attached. I had to turn him down because I'd feel obligated. But it was nice of him and I sure appreciated it."

When Bruce died, McQueen felt like he had lost a member of his family. "I cared about Bruce and I think it's going to be a great loss. I feel very bad about it. He was a wonderful guy."

Generally McQueen shunned funerals, but he did take a trip to Seattle to bid Bruce farewell. "I felt like saying goodbye to a friend. That's why I went up there to pay respect and try to make it easier on the people around him."

James Lee holds a board which is quickly turned into kindling by a powerful Bruce Lee kick.

Death of a Dear Friend

20

Early one Saturday morning in late December, 1972, I had a long distance phone call from Hong Kong. "Jimmy just died," Bruce Lee's voice choked. "Just wanna let you know (pause), excuse me I have to hang up . . . can't talk now," he apologized, apparently broken up by his friend's death.

James Lee of Oakland, California, was one of Bruce's dearest friends. Although both had the same surname, they were not related. Personality-wise, both men were very different. Where Bruce was vivacious with a quick and charming smile, James was the opposite. He spoke brashly with a stern look, hardly smiling. He had piercing eyes that could keep a person petrified by his stare. James was a heavy drinker while Bruce was an abstainer.

Although James was almost 20 years older than Bruce, they were like brothers with James taking the role of the younger brother. Bruce dictated and James followed.

James Lee had a early interest in physical endeavors. As a kid he took up wrestling and gymnastics in high school. Later, he became a weight-lifter and an amateur boxer. Before he met Bruce, he had already studied *jujitsu* and *sil lum* kung fu. Physically, he paid dearly for the years in jujit-su. He dislocated both shoulders which left a small lump on each shoulder blade.

In 1959 he met Bruce shortly after Bruce's arrival in the U.S., but didn't become his student until 1962. Since then, he had abandoned all of his other activities except for weightlifting, which he continued until his death.

Bruce's first visit to San Francisco was short as he moved to Seattle to continue his education, but both men kept in touch. In 1964, Bruce quit school (University of Washington in Seattle) with only a year left and came to live with James. James' wife was stricken with cancer then. Bruce and his new bride, Linda, spent six months with them, offering physical as well as spiritual comfort. Linda also took care of James' two children.

During this time James and Bruce became partners and opened up their own *kwoon* (school) in Oakland. James, meanwhile, started his own mail order business called, Oriental Book Sales. He published a few books and one of them was a book on Bruce Lee's technique of wing chun. Just a limited amount, about 1,000, was printed.

Bruce's fame was spreading rapidly on the West Coast. Meanwhile, his exploits were highly exaggerated, such as, "a young kung fu expert from Hong Kong has a remarkable keen sense, he fights blindfolded and is still able to block punches and kicks." Later, I realized that people were referring to Bruce's demonstration of the *chi sao* (sticky-hand) exercise in which he often blindfolded himself.

After the death of James' wife, Bruce and Linda moved to Los Angeles but both men continued to contact each other. James usually came down two or three times a year to visit, especially on special occasions like Bruce's birthday in November.

In the summer of 1972 Bruce decided to publish a book on wing chun

The tireless star in a thoughtful moment.

kung fu with Ohara Publications. I was then the publisher of that company. Bruce didn't want to use his name because the art was so different from his jeet kune do. Instead he was planning to use an alias. A few years earlier, Bruce had intended to write a book and had compiled over 1,000 photos of his art—jeet kune do. But he decided not to have the book published, fearing that some unscrupulous instructors would use it to exploit the public.

After his death, his widow, Linda, utilized those photos, realizing that it would be a crime if nothing were done with them. Bruce's knowledge would have been buried with him forever. In late 1975 I started on the project. It took almost a full year to complete the four volumes of *Bruce Lee's Fighting Method.*

Even though Bruce decided not to use his name or photos in the wing chun book, he put his whole heart and energy into its production. Conveniently, during that period, James was on a lengthy sick leave from his welding job and came to visit Bruce. James and Ted Wong were exclusively used to illustrate the techniques. For two weeks Bruce and both men worked from morning until night, Monday through Friday. "Bruce never quit," recalled Ed Ikuta, the photographer. "He just kept going and everything had to be precisely right."

Bruce was a tireless and demanding person. But he also clowned around a lot between the shootings which kept everybody in high spirits throughout the project.

Before the book went to the printer, Bruce learned that recovery for his friend James would be slow and also learned that he was almost broke. His savings was rapidly being depleted and his medical costs were skyrocketing. He was having problems collecting on-the-job medical expenses from his company.

"Damn company said I didn't get sick from the job," James complained. "My job is to weld inside huge drums. Even with a mask on, I still can smell the fumes. That's how I got sick."

Although Bruce could really have used the money from the book since he hadn't completely recovered from his back injury and also an addition to the family (daughter Shannon), he nevertheless pitied his friend and handed over the title to James without a second thought. "Can you do me a favor and give Jimmy the advance (royalty) right away?" he asked me. "He needs the bread more than me."

Bruce didn't realize then how sick James really was and continued to train with him to the limit. I remember one day, both stopped by my office and Bruce, pointing his finger at James laughed, "Jimmy just threw up while going down Mulholland."

"Goddamit Bruce. He gives me a workout and thinks it's funny when I got a headache and began to vomit," complained James.

"What did he do to you?" I asked.

"He kicked the hell out of me!"

"Hey Bruce," I voiced my opinion, "do you know that Jimmy may have had a concussion from the blows."

James Lee demonstrating breaking.

Bruce just shrugged his shoulders and smiled mischieviously, "For a guy over 50, he's in pretty good shape. He can take it."

Before the book was out, Bruce left for Thailand to do a movie and didn't return until early fall. He came back to act in three more episodes of TV's *Longstreet*, and also had to sell his home in Bel Air as he was planning to live in Hong Kong. Although his time was very limited, he still took a day off to see his pal in Oakland.

I still remember it was just three months before when the three of us had lunch in a Japanese restaurant in the suburbs of Los Angeles. That day was hot and unusually smoggy. There was a lot of kidding and laughing among us. Even a first-alert smog couldn't have dampened our spirits then. Nothing could have disturbed us at that moment. Bruce was about to leave for Thailand for his biggest role.

Grinning ecstatically, Jimmy slapped Bruce's back and said, "Boy, I'm real happy for you, Bruce!"

Bruce responded with a light slap on his own chest and raised his clenched fist. "This is it! This guy's gonna make it this time," he laughed loudly. "I can just feel it in my bones and I know I'm gonna make it."

That short three-month span changed the lives of both men. Bruce was on cloud nine. His first movie was a tremendous success and his just-released second movie was zipping to another record. He became the newest idol in the Far East.

The day he returned from Oakland, I joined Bruce at the Beverly Hills Hotel. He stayed in one of the $100-a-day bungalows which gave him a good deal of privacy. It was surrounded with bushes, trees and flowers. The oak leaves were turning yellow then, I recall. The warmth from the sun's rays felt good. It was one of the most beautiful days I'd ever seen in Southern California. The sky was completely blue with not a single trace of cloud. No smog. The birds were chirping away as they hopped from branch to branch. The breeze kept us comfortable as it rustled through the trees.

"How's Jimmy?" I asked. His jaw dropped, his cheery face turned to grief. "He looks real bad. He's just skin and bones. That poor guy just told me that he has cancer of the lung. Don't think he's gonna live long and he knows it too.

"Dammit, I wish I had some bread sooner," cried Bruce. "I may have been able to save his life." Bruce invited James to his next premiere of *Way of the Dragon* (released as *Return of the Dragon* in most countries). "Jimmy never traveled much and I felt that's the least I could do for him. If the doctor allows him, he should be in Hong Kong for Christmas. You know, I'd like to have him with me but I don't know how much time I can afford. I've been so busy; I hardly had any time, even to sleep. You know sometimes I only have three hours of sleep a night. That's why I lost so much weight.

"Another thing that is bugging me—what would happen if he should die there? Man, how am I gonna ship his body back? There's so much red tape trying to ship a corpse between countries. How could I find the time?

"But the most difficult part is to say goodbye to someone so close when I known darn well it'll be the last time I'm gonna see him. Just think, I'm not gonna see him again—ever—after that day," he continued with tears in his eyes. "Boy, I'm emotional that way and I don't know how to take it. It's just gonna break me up. Right now, I'm already down . . . I hate to face that day," he stammered uncontrollably.

At that instant we were oblivious of our surrounding. We couldn't hear the birds chirping. Nor notice the blue sky. Nor feel the warmth of the sun's rays. Nor enjoy the beautiful sunset that day.

Until Bruce's explanation, I didn't know what to think of James. He used to write to me and his letters were hardly legible but I could make them out. He seemed to be so desperate. He wanted to amass a fortune overnight. He was coming up with all kinds of ideas and wanted me to reprint Bruce's first book, but Bruce was against it. "James Lee's reprints of my first book, I do not approve as it is going against my principle," Bruce wrote on July 24, 1972, from Hong Kong.

I guessed James wanted to leave something for his two children as he realized they couldn't count on anyone to help them. Both of them still had so much more schooling ahead of them. He was just a desperate man who learned that his time was near and wanted to leave something for his kids.

Bruce's dilemma was short-lived as the doctor forbade James to travel. He spent his Christmas in Oakland that year but failed to see New Year's Day. He died in his home alone. "I got real pissed off when I heard Jimmy died without anyone at his home," Bruce complained to me later. "Someone should have kept an eye on him."

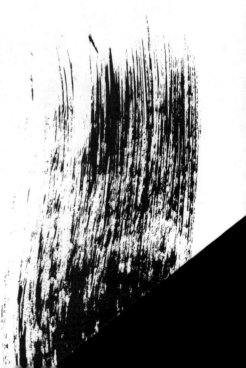

...ned to form around Bruce Lee wherever he went, but he dealt with it with poise and courtesy.

Loss of Privacy

21

"I don't understand Big Lew (referring to Lew Alcindor who is now known as Kareem Abdul-Jabbar)," Bruce Lee commented to me one day. "When kids come up for an autograph, he tries to get rid of them. Sometimes he was very rude and would just tell the kids to wait. But before the kids had a chance to catch him, he would take off."

But Bruce had a better opinion of Steve McQueen's attitude toward the public. "Steve just avoided going out. He'd either stay home or go to the desert to ride his bike."

Bruce tried many times to get McQueen to go with him to martial arts tournaments, but succeeded only once or twice. And that wasn't until after Bruce had gotten assurance from the promoter that he would not announce McQueen's presence.

James Coburn, on the other hand, was more outgoing. He attended tournaments—large or small—and didn't mind being announced. He didn't hesitate to sign autographs nor meet the people.

As Bruce's fame began to grow, he started to understand McQueen's reasoning for avoiding public places and also Jabbar's behavior with kids and adults. "In the beginning," Bruce explained, "I didn't mind all the publicity I was getting. I thought it was fun signing autographs and getting all the attention. But soon, it became a tedious chore answering the same questions over and over again, posing for photographs with strangers and forcing a smile."

Bruce mentioned that later when he, himself, became more known it became a headache getting all the attention. "Whenever I go to a public place—like a restaurant—I try to sneak in without being noticed and go directly to a corner table and sit down. I have to sit facing the wall so my back's to the crowd and eat with my head real low. Yeh, it may seem crazy," he laughed, "but that's the only way I can eat my meal in peace. You see, if I'm recognized, I'm dead. I can't eat and sign autographs at the same time. I can't just brush people off like some of those other guys do. Besides, I feel if I can make someone happy, especially a kid, by just taking a second to sign my autograph, then why not do it?"

Bruce mentioned that Hong Kong's public is not like the public in the U.S. "If you're a star and just one person recognizes you, he'll point a finger at you and everybody will just cease whatever they're doing and stare at you. They'll stare for a long time until you go away. It's almost impossible to merge into a crowd without causing a commotion."

One night Bruce attended his *The Big Boss* movie to learn the reaction of the audience. He purposely waited until the movie had started so he could sneak in when it was dark and avoid being recognized. "The usherette took me to a seat and I was so pleased with myself that no one had noticed me. But a few minutes later, the usherette shined her flashlight into my face and asked for my autograph," Bruce smiled.

As Bruce's fame grew, he began to lose his privacy more and more. Eventually, he behaved like McQueen. "The only time I go out is when I have to. Jogging early morning in Hong Kong gives me some privacy. It's sure refreshing. I don't think anyone will try to run after me for an

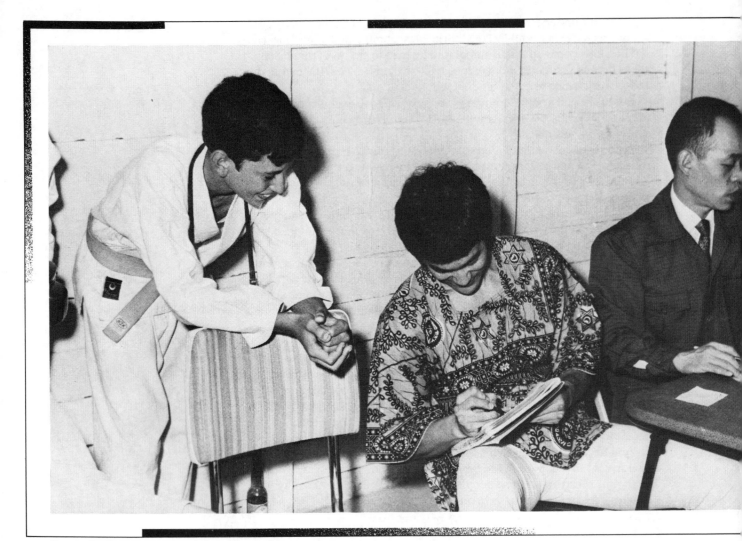

Bruce signing an autograph for a young fan.

autograph because he won't be able to keep up with me," he laughed.

Before Bruce's popularity spread to the United States, he wanted to return, "I find peace here. I'm free. I'm like anyone else here and can go any place I want without being stopped," Bruce mentioned to me. "Life is so funny. When you're struggling and trying your best to be somebody, you don't think much about privacy. All you think about is becoming wealthy and famous. But once you're there, it's not all that rosy. You crave for the old days when you could attend any kind of function and stay as long as you like and nobody bothered you."

Bruce complained that he couldn't even enjoy a movie anymore. "I have to sneak in when the movie has already started and I have to leave before it's finished. It's like reading a book with the first and last chapters missing. You don't know what's really happening and you don't know what had happened."

Even before he became a star, Bruce avoided social gatherings whenever possible. "I'm not that kind of a cat. I don't drink or smoke and those events are many times senseless. I don't like to wear stuffy clothing and be where everyone is trying to impress each other. Now, I'm not saying I'm modest, I just rather be around a few friends and talk informally about things like boxing and the martial arts.

A young man gets Kato's signature.

In all the years that I knew Bruce, he never mentioned his acting career as a child in Hong Kong. I guess to him it wasn't any great accomplishment. He was more proud of his role in the *Green Hornet* than all the prior films he made in Hong Kong.

Many felt that Bruce's success (in Hong Kong) was because he was a local product. However many, including Bruce, felt it was because the *Green Hornet* played in Hong Kong repeatedly for months after it disappeared from the tube in the U.S. It didn't bring him stardom but it opened the door for him.

"I guess I'm the only guy who ventured away from there and became an actor. To most people, including the actors and actresses from Hong Kong and Taiwan, Hollywood is like a magic kingdom. It's beyond everyone's reach and when I made it, they thought I'd accomplished an incredible feat. But if my success was based on these two facts alone, then why is it that my movies were box-office smashes in Singapore, the Philippines and other countries I haven't even visited.

When Bruce returned to Hong Kong in 1968, he was already somewhat of a celebrity there because of the *Green Hornet* series. From the time he got off the airplane, he was hounded by reporters. "It sure was an experience. I made several appearances with the largest radio and television stations. People flocked around me wherever I went. Many of them didn't even know my name, but they recognized my face. Although I wasn't paid for these appearances, I was rewarded in other ways."

The news media didn't forget Bruce after that. They followed his progress very closely even while he lived in the States. When Bruce finally signed up for his first movie, *The Big Boss*, he had a bigger voice than he normally would have had when he signed his contract with the producer,

Raymond Chow of Golden Harvest. Besides, he was also given some freedom to direct, especially the fight scenes.

Being a big star wasn't easy for Bruce. The media hounded not only Bruce but his family. Small incidents or conversations were greatly exaggerated. Even Bruce's kids had to be protected for fear of saying the wrong things.

Bruce had the biggest problem though. His popularity attracted all types of people. "I had a heck of a problem after my second movie *(Fists of Fury)* became a smash. I had people stop at my door and just pass me a check for $200,000. When I asked them what it was for they replied, 'Don't worry about it, it's just a gift to you.' I didn't even know these people—they were complete strangers."

After awhile, Bruce became confused with all the offers and began to become suspicious of everyone. "It was very bewildering. I didn't know who to trust and I even grew suspicious of my old pals. I was in a period when I didn't know who was trying to take advantage of me.

"When people just pass out big money—just like that," continued the wiry star, "you don't know what to think. I destroyed all the checks but it was difficult to do, because I didn't know what they were for."

Like the stars in Hollywood, Bruce also encountered the same type of problems in Hong Kong. Prior to his death it was rumored that one of the Chinese actresses was his mistress. The story made headlines in Hong Kong but Bruce wasn't too concerned because Linda, his wife, understood that this was part of his occupation. When I asked Bruce about it, he said that an actress he worked with in a movie did attempt suicide once on account of him but he couldn't understand why. "That dumb girl took several pills and said that she's in love with me and gonna kill herself if she can't have me. Shit, I can't do much in that kind of situation. There's too many crazy people."

The media also played it up that the same actress "confessed that Bruce brought her a Mercedes." But Jhoon Rhee, a close friend of Bruce's, laughed when he first heard this. "Bruce buying a car for an actress?" Rhee looked at me with a twinkle in his eyes and said, "You and I know how Bruce handled his money. You know he'd never buy a car for anyone except Linda or for someone in his immediate family. Those stories are just a bunch of bull."

Although stardom did create almost an unbearable hardship to a guy like Bruce, it also gave Bruce an opportunity to help the kids in Hong Kong. Like Jim Kelly, the actor, once said, "Bruce was good for the kids. Hong Kong never had a hero for the kids, and they finally found one in Bruce. He always took the time for autographs and had good rapport with them."

Bruce was always nice to youngsters even in the U.S. Once while he was visiting me at the office, a couple of kids about nine or ten years-old stopped by to buy some magazines. When Bruce spotted them, he went quickly over and began to rap with them and slapped their hands in a friendly gesture.

When one of the office workers asked those kids if they had seen Bruce on television before, they stared at him and shook their heads. "He was Kato on the *Green Hornet*," she blurted out. The expression on their faces brought a big smile to Bruce.

"Nah! He can't be Kato!" they cried.

The office worker had to look for one of the old copies of BLACK BELT magazine to convince those kids.

But Bruce was a bigger hero to the Hong Kong kids. "I can relate to those kids," he explained. "I was brought up in Hong Kong and kids there have nothing to look forward to. The white kids (British) have all the best jobs and the rest of us had to work for them. That's why most of the kids become punks. Life in Hong Kong is so bad. Kids in the slums can never get out."

...son, Brandon.

A Maturing Family Man

"I think I'm the luckiest guy in the world," Bruce Lee told me one day. "I've got a wonderful wife who is always there when I need her, and she's a good mother, too," Bruce smiled contentedly.

Since first meeting Bruce and Linda in 1967, I felt their relationship was pretty stable. Linda was always busy, running errands, taking care of the house and their son, Brandon. Whenever we came to visit, she was always cordial—never in a bad mood. She took time to greet us and immediately went about her business, leaving us alone with Bruce.

Bruce generally dominated conversations with Linda and guests. During our workout sessions, Linda sometimes would bring cold drinks or hot tea. Occasionally she would join us and demonstrate her wing chun techniques.

Linda always pitched in to help Bruce with his day-to-day dealings such as taking phone calls when Bruce didn't want to speak to the party. Linda took care of most all family matters while Bruce concentrated on the demands of his film career.

A few years ago I asked Linda privately if she ever argued with Bruce or refused to do him favors. "Me? Argue with Bruce? You must be kidding!" she smiled. "You know I couldn't win."

Bruce, being a health nut, believed that Linda should exercise. While living in Hong Kong, Bruce had Linda join a health club where she swam daily. "All the years I've been with Linda, she was always busy. Now that we can afford to hire help, I finally got her to take it easy. We have enough servants and maids to do the housework," he told me.

Father and son go toe to toe.

Sometimes Bruce would come up with the most peculiar ideas. One evening, while they were living in Culver City, he had Linda join him in jogging. Linda had not jogged before, but she was willing. "She's OK," he said. "I had her running with me and you know, she did a full mile with my help. Whenever she wanted to stop to catch her breath, I kept urging her on."

I saw a change in Linda's personality when Bruce became a superstar. She started to be more open and stylish. She did not hesitate to give her opinion especially when they pertained to the children's welfare.

Was Bruce a good family man? He was a good husband to Linda. I never heard any cross words being exchanged between them in all the years I knew them. I think Bruce matured immensely because of the children.

After Shannon was born, Bruce became more attentive. It seemed as if his whole attitude toward family life had changed. "I have to be more concerned for them now," I recall him saying. "First time in my life I am worried about where the money will come from if anything happens to me." This was the period when he had injured his back and was recuperating in bed. His savings were low and he was in no condition to work.

From the day Shannon was born, she was the apple of his eye and Bruce paid a great deal of attention to her. One day he came to my office and was quite depressed. "I feel real bad today," he confided, "I was clipping my daughter's nails and accidentally cut her finger. When she started to scream and I saw the blood dripping, I went crazy. I didn't know what to

Bruce and Brandon practice their kicks.

...non.

do. Lucky that Linda was around. Man, I felt really bad. She's so tiny and I had to hurt her.''

As Brandon became of school age, Linda placed him in a Chinese school which she was also attending. In a few weeks he was already causing commotion in school. ''Brandon is the biggest and only white kid in his class. And we're already getting complaints that he's beating up on the other kids,'' Bruce proudly mentioned to me. I guess his son's behavior brought back memories of himself. As a child, according to his mother Grace, Bruce was an ornery kid always getting into trouble. Linda was rather perturbed by Bruce's attitude at that moment.

Bruce spent his time with his buddies frequently. Although his interests were limited, he enjoyed the company of his martial arts friends, his students and those in the movie industry. He didn't visit other martial arts schools as many had rumored. He always felt that the other martial artists' techniques were inferior to his and he didn't feel that he could gain anything. Sometimes, he attended karate tournaments, not that he enjoyed them, but to point out to his guests the faults of each contestant's techniques.

Bruce used to enjoy Chinese kung fu and Japanese sword-fighting films. His favorite was *The Blind Swordsman*. I swear he must have seen all the different versions of that movie. But his favorite pastime was to visit friends and just talk about fighting. He wasn't really the party type. Occasionally Bruce would attend exclusive parties thrown by some actors or Hollywood moguls. However, when he threw a party himself, he only invited his martial arts friends and students.

Whenever Bruce was selected to be honored by some organization, usually from the Chinese community, he politely refused. He never believed in collecting plaques, trophies or medals and, I don't remember ever seeing any in his home. He was more proud of his collection of ancient books and boxing films.

The only time I remember him accepting such an honor was in 1970 when he was invited to be the Grand Marshal in a parade in a small midwest town. ''I went because I thought it would help popularize *Green Hornet* and besides, I got paid five grand.''

As Bruce matured, his attitude toward his children changed. He talked about them more often with pride. During his last trip to the U.S., Bruce proudly showed me a clipping that was written by his son, Brandon, in a Hong Kong newspaper. But Linda was not too pleased with all the limelight their children were getting. ''I hope we can return to Los Angeles as soon as possible. The kids can't have a normal life here,'' she emphasized directing her comments to Bruce.

When Bruce married, it wasn't with the blessing of Linda's mother. But his relationship with his mother-in-law improved greatly through the years. But the best years between the two were when Bruce became a superstar. Bruce invited Linda's mother to Hong Kong and she really had a great time. ''She was so proud of me,'' Bruce smiled glowingly, ''because wherever we went, we were given the V.I.P. treatment. I guess that's the first time in her life she had that kind of attention."

It was Linda's aunt who opposed their marriage more than anyone else. She didn't believe in mixed marriages. She said that, according to the Bible, mixed marriages were sinful. I don't think Bruce had any problem with his side of the family in that his mother was part Caucasian.

According to Bruce's mother Grace, his father had very little to do with his family. She said that her husband was close to the children when they were young. But as the children got older, her husband changed and became a traditional Chinese father. He became heavily preoccupied with his work and his studies. "He spent most of his time in his room studying or sleeping and didn't sit with the family except at meals."

Bruce respected his older brother Peter. I think Bruce looked up to those with athletic ability more than any other asset. Peter had been Hong Kong's fencing champion for several years and even participated in the Olympics. It was through Peter, that Bruce learned his shuffling movement and stance of jeet kune do.

Bruce was critical toward his young brother because Robert had no athletic inclination. "Bruce used to force me to eat all kinds of protein food and sweets because he felt I was too skinny," Robert complained. "He wanted me to put on more weight and muscle. He even tried to put me on a weightlifting schedule."

As long as I knew Bruce he didn't appreciate Robert's talents. While still in his teens, Robert had already accomplished more than most adults. He had his own band, his own television show and he played over seven musical instruments, sang and composed his own music.

If Bruce had died a year or so earlier, he wouldn't have been able to provide for his family because he didn't earn enough. But, by the time of his death, he had bought enough life insurance and had set up other provisions. I really saw a different Bruce since he had gone to live in Hong Kong. Different, but a highly matured and wiser man.

Brandon gets his kicks.

Robert Lee, a professional singer-songwriter who penned tunes with his brother Bruce, and wrote songs about him after his death.

More Bruce Lee Books from Ohara

TAO OF JEET KUNE DO
by Bruce Lee. Code No. 401

BRUCE LEE'S FIGHTING METHOD Vol. 1: Self-Defense Techniques
by Bruce Lee and M. Uyehara. Code No. 402

BRUCE LEE'S FIGHTING METHOD Vol. 2: Basic Training
by Bruce Lee and M. Uyehara. Code No. 403

BRUCE LEE'S FIGHTING METHOD Vol. 3: Skill in Techniques
by Bruce Lee and M. Uyehara. Code No. 404

BRUCE LEE'S FIGHTING METHOD Vol. 4: Advanced Techniques
by Bruce Lee and M. Uyehara. Code No. 405

CHINESE GUNG FU
by Bruce Lee. Code No. 451

THE LEGENDARY BRUCE LEE
by the Editors of Black Belt magazine. *Code No. 446*

THE BRUCE LEE STORY
by Linda Lee. Code No. 460

THE INCOMPARABLE FIGHTER
by M. Uyehara. Code No. 461

OHARA ▯ PUBLICATIONS, INC., 24900 Anza Drive, Unit E Santa Clarita, California 91355